Written by:
Regina A. Bradley

Edited by:
Emily Ramsower, Laura Lundberg

Cover Design:
Peter Licalzi

Printed in the United States of America

Table of Contents

Introduction

Congratulations on your excellent decision to join the United States military! The choice to dedicate yourself to serving your country is admirable, and we want to help you do your absolute best. So what is your first step?

Getting your AFQT score.

Reviewing the material isn't always enough – we want you to be able to face your examination with complete confidence, and that includes knowing what to expect from the test itself. In this introduction, we'll give you a detailed overview of the exam and how it works, while answering any questions you may have about what the AFQT score and ASVAB test are. We'll also provide some tips as to what you will need to do to prepare for this testing process.

What is the ASVAB?

The ASVAB stands for Armed Services Vocational Aptitude Battery. It is the test you will take to determine if you are eligible to enter the military.

Then what's the AFQT? Are They The Same?

The score you are given is called your AFQT score (Armed Forces Qualification Test). The acronyms can get rather confusing, but in short: you take the ASVAB and get an AFQT score. The AFQT is not a separate exam, just the name of the score you earn.

Breaking Down the ASVAB Test

The ASVAB has 9 sections – only the first four are used to calculate your AFQT score. The other sections are used as indicators of any extra skills you might have that would make you a strong candidate for certain specialized positions; but don't worry - they don't have any bearing on whether or not you are qualified to enlist.

The Nine Sections of the ASVAB:
Word Knowledge (WK)
Paragraph Comprehension (PC)
Arithmetic Reasoning (AR)
Mathematics Knowledge (MK)
General Science (GS)
Auto and Shop Information (AS)
Electrical Information (EI)
Mechanical Comprehension (MC)
Assembling Objects (AO)

The Four Sections that Make Up Your AFQT Score:
Word Knowledge (WK)
Paragraph Comprehension (PC)
Arithmetic Reasoning (AR)
Mathematics Knowledge (MK)

AFQT scores range from 0-99, but that score does not represent how many questions you got right or wrong. Instead, it is a percentile score of how well you did compared to a group of standardized ASVAB test takers. So, for example - if you got a 60, that means you scored higher than 60% of that group, but 40% did better than you. All potential enlisted personnel are tested against each other, regardless of which branch you want to enter.

The U.S. Congress has a legal minimum score of 9 to qualify for the military. If you don't make at least a 9, then you cannot legally enter. However, beyond that bare minimum requirement, each branch has its own minimum standards. These are:

AIR FORCE: 36
US ARMY: 31
MARINE CORP: 32
NAVY: 35
COAST GUARD: 36

Let's use an example:

You score a 34. While you would be eligible for the Army and Marines, you would not be able to enlist to the Navy; Air Force; or Coast Guard.

Keep in mind that these values do change from time to time – so it's a good idea to check with your recruiter what scores are required in your desired branch.

So why does the military care about your math, arithmetic, word, and paragraph skills? Once in the military, you won't necessarily need to solve math equations or demonstrate perfect paragraph comprehension (although these skills are certainly useful!).

Instead, a high AFQT score shows the military that you learned and remembered skills taught to you in high school. Their thought is: if you were teachable in high school, then you will be teachable in the military. The military has a lot to teach you, so they want to make sure you are up to the challenge beforehand. That way you aren't wasting your time, and they're not wasting their time.

Getting to Know the ASVAB – Format

The ASVAB is officially called the ASVAB-CAT (though when people refer to it, they just call it "ASVAB" for short). "CAT" means Computer Adaptive Test.

The ASVAB used to be administered as a paper-and-pencil exam, but, like many things, it has become computer based. Some people believe that the new computer-based test is the same as the old pencil-and-paper version, but that isn't true!

On the old test, there were no points taken away for wrong answers, so test-takers were encouraged to guess blindly if they didn't know an answer. The new test is called the ASVAB-CAT – and the word "Adaptive" in "CAT" means that the test is customized for each person as they take the exam.

Getting to Know the ASVAB – Adaptive Tests

On the ASVAB-CAT, everyone starts off with a question of medium-level difficulty. If you get it right, then your next question will be harder. It will also be worth more points.

If, however, you get questions wrong, you will be given easier questions. That may sound nice, but the easier questions are worth fewer points.

Here is a breakdown of how this works:

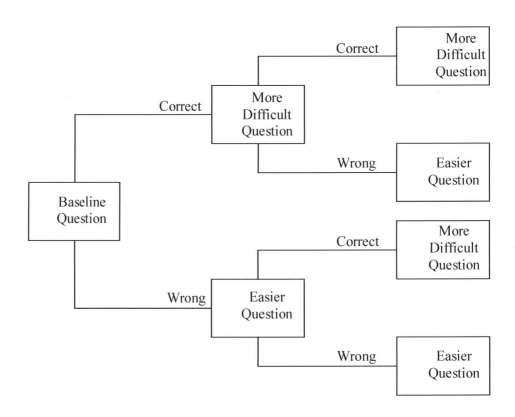

This process helps test officials score everyone more quickly and accurately – if someone misses a lot of easy questions, then they are less likely to qualify for the military.

Because of this new system, there is one HUGE difference between the ASVAB-CAT and the old test: never, ever guess! You run the risk of getting the answer incorrect, which will decrease your chances of getting more point-worthy questions.

Of course, there will be times when a question might be too difficult, and you just don't know the answer. What then? You should also know that you cannot skip questions on the ASVAB test. That doesn't mean you're stuck! If you can't figure out the answer to that question, then you need to guess.

However, this should be an *educated* guess – don't just wildly pick an answer at random. Instead, you need to do your best to narrow down your answer choices. Try to eliminate at least one or two choices; that will increase your odds of guessing correctly.

Obviously, you want to do your best on the ASVAB so that you can get a high AFQT score . Using this book is a great way to get started. It doesn't matter if you barely passed high school, or got poor grades; it doesn't matter if you feel like it's been too long since you've learned the material. This book will help you prepare. By studying efficiently for the ASVAB, you can receive a qualifying AFQT score.

Getting a good AFQT score isn't easy for everyone, but if you put your determination, dedication, and hard work into overcoming the challenges of studying, you will see amazing results.

Again, congratulations on your decision to join the military. We wish you the best in your new career, starting with a great AFQT score!

Chapter 1: Word Knowledge

The Word Knowledge subtest is one of the four core AFQT tests used to determine your eligibility to enlist. The military considers clear and concise communication so important that it is taught and graded at all levels of leadership training. If you are planning a military career, you will be tested on your verbal skills as you move through the ranks.

Your score is also used to determine if you qualify for many specialized jobs, such as military security and intelligence, air traffic control, medical, and administrative positions. The good news is that most individuals have been exposed to all of the vocabulary words used on the subtest by the time they have reached the tenth grade. This doesn't mean that you are going to recognize every single word. It *does* mean, however, that you won't be expected to know advanced Latin or graduate science terminology.

This section of the test gives you 35 questions to answer in 11 minutes. This may seem like a disproportionate amount of time – it comes out to about 18 seconds per question – but don't worry! We're going to arm you with all of the knowledge you'll need in order to work quickly and efficiently through this section.

You will encounter two types of questions on the ASVAB Word Knowledge subtest:

1. To define the word without context:

   Garner most nearly means:
   - a) Create.
   - b) Propose.
   - c) Demonstrate.
   - d) Gather.

2. To define the word within the context:

   The chemicals in the water were benign.
   - a) Natural.
   - b) Undisturbed.
   - c) Harmless.
   - d) Dangerous.

   (The correct answers are: **d) Gather** and **c) Harmless**)

VOCABULARY BASIC TRAINING

The first step in getting ready for this section of the ASVAB consists of reviewing the basic techniques used to determine the meanings of words you are not familiar with. The good news is that you have been using various degrees of these techniques since you first began to speak. Sharpening these skills will help you with the paragraph comprehension subtest.

Following each section you will find a practice drill. Use your scores on these to determine if you need to study a particular subject matter further. At the end of each section, you will find a Practice Drill to test your Knowledge.

The questions found on the practice drills are not given in the two formats found on the Word Knowledge subtest; rather they are designed to reinforce the skills needed to score well on the Word Knowledge subtest.

Context Clues

The most fundamental vocabulary skill is using the context of a word to determine its meaning. The military considers this ability of considerable importance, and it is one of the two styles of questions on this subtest. Your ability to observe sentences closely is extremely useful when it comes to understanding new vocabulary words.

Types of Context

There are two different types of context that can help you understand the meaning of unfamiliar words: **sentence context** and **situational context**. Regardless of which context is present, these types of questions are not really testing your knowledge of vocabulary; they are testing your ability to comprehend the meaning of a word through its usage.

Situational context is the basis of the Paragraph Comprehension subtest and will be discussed in chapter two.

Sentence context occurs in the sentence containing the vocabulary word. To figure out words using sentence context clues, you should first determine the most important words in the sentence.

For Example:

I had a hard time reading her illegible handwriting.
a) Neat.
b) Unsafe.
c) Sloppy.
d) Educated.

Already, you know that this sentence is discussing something that is hard to read. Look at the word that **illegible** is describing: **handwriting**. Based on context clues, you can tell that illegible means that her handwriting is hard to read.

Next, look at the answer choices. Choice **a) Neat** is obviously a wrong answer because neat handwriting would not be difficult to read. Choice **b) Unsafe** and **d) Educated** don't make sense. Therefore, choice **c) Sloppy** is the best answer choice.

Types of Clues

There are four types of clues that can help you understand the context, which in turn helps you define the word. They are **restatement**, **positive/negative**, **contrast**, and **specific detail**.

Restatement clues occur when the definition of the word is clearly stated in the sentence.

For Example:

The dog was <u>dauntless</u> in the face of danger, braving the fire to save the girl.
a) Difficult.
b) Fearless.
c) Imaginative.
d) Pleasant.

Demonstrating **bravery** in the face of danger would be **fearless,** choice **b)**. In this case, the context clues tell you exactly what the word means.

Positive/negative clues can tell you whether a word has a positive or negative meaning.

For Example:

The magazine gave a great review of the fashion show, stating the clothing   was **sublime**.
a) Horrible.
b) Exotic.
c) Bland.
d) Gorgeous.

The sentence tells us that the author liked the clothing enough to write a **great** review, so you know that the best answer choice is going to be a

12

positive word. Therefore, you can immediately rule out choices **a)** and **c)** because they are negative words. **Exotic** is a neutral word; alone, it doesn't inspire a **great** review. The most positive word is gorgeous, which makes choice **d) Gorgeous** the best answer.

The following sentence uses both restatement and positive/negative clues:

"Janet suddenly found herself <u>destitute</u>, so poor she could barely afford to eat."

The second part of the sentence clearly indicates that destitute is a negative word; it also restates the meaning: very poor.

Contrast clues include the opposite meaning of a word. Words like **but, on the other hand,** and **however** are tip-offs that a sentence contains a contrast clue.
For Example:

Beth did not spend any time preparing for the test, but Tyron kept a <u>rigorous</u> study schedule.
   a) Strict.
   b) Loose.
   c) Boring.
   d) Strange.

In this case, the word **but** tells us that Tyron studied in a different way than Beth. If Beth did not study very hard, then Tyron did study hard for the test. The best answer here, therefore, is choice **a) Strict**.

Specific detail clues give a precise detail that can help you understand the meaning of the word.
   For Example:

The box was heavier than he expected and it began to become <u>cumbersome</u>.
   a) Impossible.
   b) Burdensome.
   c) Obligated.
   d) Easier.

Start by looking at the specific details of the sentence. Choice **d)** can be eliminated right away because it is doubtful it would become **easier** to carry something that is **heavier**. There are also no clues in the sentence to indicate he was **obligated** to carry the box, so choice **c)** can also be disregarded. The sentence specifics, however, do tell you that the package was cumbersome because it was heavy to carry; something heavy to carry is a burden, which is **burdensome**, choice **b)**.

It is important to remember that more than one of these clues can be present in the same sentence. The more there are, the easier it will be to determine the meaning of the word, so look for them.

Denotation and Connotation

As you know, many English words have more than one meaning. For example, the word **quack** has two distinct definitions: the sound a duck makes; and a person who publicly pretends to have a skill, knowledge, education, or qualification which they do not possess.

The **denotations** of a word are the dictionary definitions.

The **connotations** of a word are the implied meaning(s) or emotion which the word makes you think.

For Example:

"Sure," Pam said excitedly, "I'd just love to join your club; it sounds so exciting!"

Now, read this sentence:

"Sure," Pam said sarcastically, "I'd just love to join your club; it sounds so exciting!"

Even though the two sentences only differ by one word, they have completely different meanings. The difference, of course, lies in the words "excitedly" and "sarcastically."

Look back to the underlined word – **reinforce** - on page 12. Can you think of several words that could be used and the sentence have the same meaning?

PRACTICE DRILL – VOCABULARY BASIC TRAINING
Use context clues to determine the meaning of each underlined word.

1. His story didn't seem very realistic; even though it was a documentary.
   a) Believable.
   b) Humorous.
   c) Poetic.
   d) Exciting.

2. Listening to music too loudly, especially through headphones, can impair your hearing.
   a) Damage.
   b) Heighten.
   c) Use.
   d) Ensure.

3. Kelly's game happened to coincide with the Sue's recital.
   a) Happen before.
   b) Occur at the same time.
   c) Occur afterward.
   d) Not happen.

4. The weather has been very extreme lately; thankfully, today it's much more temperate.
   a) Troubling.
   b) Beautiful.
   c) Cold.
   d) Moderate.

5. He knew he couldn't win the race after falling off his bike, so he had to concede.
   a) Continue.
   b) Give up.
   c) Challenge.
   d) Be thankful.

6. The editor, preferring a more terse writing style, cut 30% of the words from the article.
   a) Elegant.
   b) Factual.
   c) Descriptive.
   d) Concise.

7. Victor Frankenstein spent the last years of his life chasing his <u>elusive</u> monster, which was always one step ahead.
    a) Unable to be compared.
    b) Unable to be captured.
    c) Unable to be forgotten.
    d) Unable to be avoided.

8. Certain <u>passages</u> were taken from the book for the purpose of illustration.
    a) Excerpts.
    b) Contents.
    c) Paragraphs.
    d) Tables.

9. The investigator searched among the <u>ruins</u> for the cause of the fire.
    a) Terminal.
    b) Foundation.
    c) Rubble.
    d) Establishment.

10. To make her novels more engaging, Cynthia was known to <u>embellish</u> her writing with fictitious details.
    a) Add to.
    b) Detract.
    c) Isolate.
    d) Disavow.

11. Robert's well-timed joke served to <u>diffuse</u> the tension in the room and the party continued happily.
    a) Refuse.
    b) Intensify.
    c) Create.
    d) Soften.

12. I had a difficult time understanding the book because the author kept <u>digressing</u> to unrelated topics.
    a) Deviating, straying.
    b) Regressing, reverting.
    c) Changing the tone.
    d) Expressing concisely.

13. The senator <u>evaded</u> almost every question.
- a) Avoided.
- b) Answered indirectly.
- c) Refused to answer directly.
- d) Deceived.

14. Sammie hasn't come out of her room all afternoon, but I would <u>surmise</u> that it is because she is upset about not being able to go to the mall.
- a) Confirm.
- b) Surprise.
- c) Believe.
- d) Guess.

15. The details can be worked out later; what's important is that the company follows the <u>crux</u> of the argument, which is that everyone be paid equally.
- a) Overall tone.
- b) Specific fact.
- c) Main point.
- d) Logic, reasoning.

Use context clues to choose the best word to complete the sentence.

16. Mr. Collins _____ tomatoes so vehemently that he felt ill just smelling them.
- a) Resented.
- b) Disliked.
- c) Detested.
- d) Hated.

17. We were rolling on the ground with laughter during the _____ new movie.
- a) Comical.
- b) Humorous.
- c) Amusing.
- d) Hilarious.

18. Tina's parents made us feel right at home during our visit to their house with their generous _____.
- a) Unselfishness
- b) Politeness
- c) Hospitality
- d) Charity

19. Although his mother was not happy that he broke the window, she was pleased that he was _____ about it.

    a) Honest.

    b) Trustworthy.

    c) Authentic.

    d) Decent.

20. The soldiers _____ to their feet immediately when then officer walked into the room.

    a) Stood.

    b) Leapt.

    c) Rose.

    d) Skipped.

ANSWERS – VOCABULARY BASIC TRAINING

1. **a) Believable.** Realistic means accurate, truthful, and believable.

2. **a) Damage.** This is the only logical choice.

3. **b) Occur at the same time.** According to information in the sentence, the game was scheduled at the same time as the recital.

4. **d) Moderate.** The context says that the weather has been "extreme." It does not say if the weather has been extremely hot or cold; therefore, choices **b) Beautiful** and **c) Cold** can be ruled out. The sentence also indicates a change from negative to positive making moderate the best choice.

5. **b) Give up.** The speaker of the sentence knows they cannot win, so choice **b)** is the best choice.

6. **d) Concise.** Terse means concise, using no unnecessary words. The main clue is that the editor cut words from the article, reducing its wordiness.

7. **b) Unable to be captured.** Elusive means evasive, difficult to capture.

8. **a) Excerpt.** An excerpt is a passage or quote from a book, article, or other publication

9. **c) Rubble** is synonymous with ruin.

10. **a) Add to.** To embellish is to add details to a story to make it more appealing.

11. **d) Soften.** The clues *tension* and *continue happily* tell you that **d)** is the best choice

12. **a) To deviate, stray.** To digress means to deviate; to stray from the main subject in writing or speaking.

13. **a) To avoid.** To evade means to avoid by cleverness. The senator avoids answering the question by changing the subject.

14. **d) Guess.** The speaker is guessing why Samantha is upset based on circumstances; she has not actually given a reason.

15. **c) Main point.** Crux means the central or main point, especially of a problem. The main context clue is that the speaker isn't concerned with the details but is focused on getting agreement on the main point.

16. c) Detested. The knowledge that Mr. Collins feels ill just smelling tomatoes suggests that his hatred for tomatoes is intense; therefore, the best choice will be the most negative. To **dislike** tomatoes – choice **b)** – is the most neutral word, so this choice can be ruled out. **Resented** is a word that generally applies to people or their actions, ruling out choice **a)**. Given the choice between **c)** and **d),** the most negative is **c) Detested**.

17. d) Hilarious. The movie must be extremely funny for the audience to have this sort of reaction, and, while all of the answer choices are synonyms for funny, the only one that means extremely funny is choice **d) Hilarious**.

18. c) Hospitality. Although all four choices describe different types of kindness, **unselfishness** – choice **a)** – can be ruled out because it has the same basic meaning as the adjective, generous. Choice **d) Charity** is a kindness usually associated with those less fortunate; since nothing in the context indicates this type of relationship, this choice can also be eliminated. Left with choices **b) Politeness** and **c) Hospitality**, hospitality best describes the kindness of welcoming someone into your home.

19. a) Honest. Again we have a case in which all of the word choices are synonyms for the word honest. In this case, the most neutral word is the best choice. Choice **b) Trustworthy, c) Authentic**, and **d) Decent** do not make as much sense as the most basic synonym, **honest**.

20. b) Leapt. The word immediately is the main clue. **a) Stood** and **c) Rose** are neutral words that do not convey a sense of urgency. Choice **b) Leapt** is the only word that implies the immediacy demanded by the sentence context.

ROOTS, PREFIXES, and SUFFIXES

Word Knowledge questions will also require you to determine the meaning of a word without sentence context. Although you are not expected to know every word in the English language, you are expected to have the ability to use deductive reasoning to find the choice that is the best match for the word in question, which is why we are going to explain how to break a word into its parts of meaning

prefix – root – suffix

One trick in dividing a word into its parts is to first divide the word into its **syllables**. To show how syllables can help you find roots and affixes, we'll use the word **descendant,** which means one who comes from an ancestor. Start by dividing the word into its individual syllables; this word has three: **de-scend-ant**. The next step is to look at the beginning and end of the word, and then determine if these syllables are prefixes, suffixes, or possible roots. You can then use the meanings of each part to guide you in defining the word. When you divide words into their specific parts, they do not always add up to an exact definition, but you will see a relationship between their parts.

Note: This trick won't always work in every situation, because not all prefixes, roots, and suffixes have only one syllable. For example, take the word **monosyllabic** (which ironically means "one syllable"). There are five syllables in that word, but only three parts. The prefix is "mono," meaning "one." The root "syllab" refers to "syllable," while the suffix "ic" means "pertaining to." Therefore, we have one very long word which means "pertaining to one syllable."

The more familiar you become with these fundamental word parts, the easier it will be to define unfamiliar words. Although the words found on the Word Knowledge subtest are considered vocabulary words learned by the tenth grade level of high school, some are still less likely to be found in an individual's everyday vocabulary. The root and affixes list in this chapter uses more common words as examples to help you learn them more easily. Don't forget that you use word roots and affixes every day, without even realizing it. Don't feel intimidated by the long list of roots and affixes (prefixes and suffixes) at the end of this chapter, because you already know and use them every time you communicate with some else, verbally and in writing. If you take the time to read through the list just once a day for two weeks, you will be able to retain most of them and understand a high number of initially unfamiliar words.

Roots

Roots are the building blocks of all words. Every word is either a root itself or has a root. Just as a plant cannot grow without roots, neither can vocabulary, because a word must have a root to give it meaning.

For Example:

The test instructions were **unclear.**

The root is what is left when you strip away all the prefixes and suffixes from a word. In this case, take away the prefix "un-", and you have the root **clear.**

Roots are not always recognizable words, because they generally come from Latin or Greek words., such as **nat**, a Latin root meaning **born**. The word native, which means a person born of a referenced placed, comes from this root, so does the word prenatal, meaning before birth. Yet, if you used the prefix **nat** instead of born, just on its own, no one would know what you were talking about.

Words can also have more than one root. For example, the word **omnipoten**t means all powerful. Omnipotent is a combination of the roots **omni-**, meaning all or every, and -**potent**, meaning power or strength. In this case, **omni** cannot be used on its own as a single word, but **potent** can.

Again, it is important to keep in mind that roots do not always match the exact definitions of words and they can have several different spellings, but breaking a word into its parts is still one of the best ways to determine its meaning.

PRACTICE DRILL - ROOTS
Try to find the root in each of the underlined words.

1. The bridge was out, so the river was <u>impassable</u>.
    - a) Im-
    - b) -pass-
    - c) -a-
    - d) –able

2. I am usually on time, but my husband is <u>chronically</u> late.
    - a) Chron-
    - b) -chronical-
    - c) -ally-
    - d) -ic

3. The only way to succeed is by <u>striving</u> to do your best.
    - a) Str-
    - b) Striv-
    - c) Strive-
    - d) -ing

4. We drifted along lazily on the <u>tranquil</u> river.
    - a) Tra-
    - b) -qui-
    - c) Tranq-
    - d) -uil

5. A <u>pediatrician</u> is a doctor who takes care of children.
- a) Ped-
- b) -ia-
- c) -tri-
- d) -cian

Choose the word that shares the same root as the given word.

6. Audible
- a) Auditorium.
- b) Because.
- c) Dribble.
- d) Bagel.

7. Nominate
- a) Eaten.
- b) Minute.
- c) Hated.
- d) Synonym.

8. Disappoint
- a) Disappear.
- b) Appointment.
- c) Interest.
- d) Potato.

9. Dilute
- a) Flute.
- b) Dictate.
- c) Pollute.
- d) Hesitate.

10. Sympathy
- a) System.
- b) Empathy.
- c) Pattern.
- d) Rhythm.

11. Science
- a) Conscious.
- b) Once.
- c) Alien.
- d) Parasite.

12. Incline
- a) Recline.
- b) Independent.
- c) Cluster.
- d) Twine.

For each question below, use the Latin word root to determine the meaning of the underlined word.

13. An amiable person is:
- a) Talkative, loud.
- b) Truthful, honest.
- c) Highly educated.
- d) Friendly, good-natured.

14. A lucid argument:
- a) Is very clear and intelligible.
- b) Is loosely held together, tenuous.
- c) Frequently digresses.
- d) Errs repeatedly in its logic.

15. A complacent person:
- a) Frequently makes mistakes, but does not accept responsibility.
- b) Likes to pick fights.
- c) Is contented to a fault, self-satisfied.
- d) Is known to tell lies, embellish the truth.

16. To exacerbate a problem means:
- a) To solve it.
- b) To analyze it.
- c) To lessen it.
- d) To worsen it.

17. To measure the veracity of something is to measure its:
- a) Value or worth.
- b) Truthfulness.
- c) Weight.
- d) Life force.

18. Something that is eloquent is:
- a) Dull, trite, hackneyed.
- b) Expressed in a powerful and effective manner.
- c) Very old, antiquated.
- d) Equally divided or apportioned.

24

19. To <u>indict</u> someone is to:
    a) Pick a fight with that person.
    b) Stop or block that person from doing something.
    c) Charge that person with a crime.
    d) Love that person dearly.

20. A <u>quiescent</u> place is:
    a) Very isolated.
    b) Tumultuous, chaotic.
    c) Sacred.
    d) Still, at rest.

21. An individual with <u>equanimity</u>:
    a) Has a violent temper.
    b) Is very stubborn.
    c) Enjoys the company of others.
    d) Is even-tempered and composed.

ANSWERS – ROOTS

2. **b)** –pass-

3. **a) Chron-**

4. **c) Strive-**

5. **b)** –qui-. *Quies* is a Latin root meaning rest or quiet.

6. **a) Ped-.** *Ped* is a Latin root meaning child or education. You might recognize that the suffix **-cian** refers to what someone does, such as physician or beautician. The suffix **-iatr** relates to doctors, as you can see in the words psychiatry and podiatry. Both suffixes support the root of the word.

7. **a) Auditorium.** From the Latin root **aud,** meaning hearing or listening.

8. **d) Synonym.** The words nominate and synonym share the root, **nom,** meaning name. Remember, roots are not necessarily going to be in the same position in other words.

9. **b) Appointment.** Greek root **poie,** meaning to make.

10. **c) Pollute.** Both dilute and pollute come from the root **lut,** meaning to wash.

11. **b) Empathy.** The words sympathy and empathy come from the Greek root **path,** meaning feeling, suffering, or disease.

12. **a) Conscious.** Science and conscious share the Latin root **sci,** which means to know.

12. **a) Recline.** The words incline and recline both share the Greek root *clin,* meaning to lean toward or bend.

13. **d)** The root **am** means love. Amiable means friendly and agreeable or good natured, likeable, or pleasing.

14. **a)** The root **luc/lum/lus** means light. Lucid means very clear, easy to understand, intelligible.

15. **c)** The root **plac** means to please. Complacent means contented to a fault; self-satisfied (pleased with oneself).

16. **d)** The root **ac** means sharp, bitter. To exacerbate means to make worse or to increase the severity, violence, or bitterness of.

17. **b)** The root **ver** means truth. Veracity means truth or truthfulness.

18. **b)** The root **loc/log/loqu** means word or speech. Eloquent means expressed in a powerful, fluent, and persuasive manner.

19. **c)** The root **dic/dict/dit** means to say, tell, or use words. To indict means to formally accuse of or charge with a crime.

20. **d)** The root **qui** means quiet. Quiescent means inactive, quiet, or at rest.

21. **d)** The root **equ** means equal or even. Equanimity means calmness of temperament, even-temperedness, or patience and composure, especially under stress.

Prefixes and Suffixes

Prefixes are syllables added to the beginning of a word and suffixes are syllables added to the end of the word. Both carry assigned meanings. The common name for prefixes and suffixes is **affixes**. Affixes do not have to be attached directly to a root and a word can often have more than one prefix and/or suffix. Prefixes and suffixes can be attached to a word to completely change the word's meaning or to enhance the word's original meaning. Although they don't mean much to us on their own, when attached to other words affixes can make a world of difference.

We can use the word **prefix** as an example:

Fix means to place something securely.
Pre means before.
Prefix means to place something before or in front.

An example of a suffix:

Femin is a root. It means female, woman.
-ism means act, practice or process.
Feminism is the defining and establishing of equal political, economic, and social rights for women.

Unlike prefixes, **suffixes** can be used to change a word's part of speech.
For example, take a look at these sentences:

Randy raced to the finish line.
Shana's costume was very racy.

In the first sentence, raced is a verb. In the second sentence, racy is an adjective. By changing the suffix from **-ed** to **-y**, the word race changes from a verb into an adjective, which has an entirely different meaning.

Although you cannot determine the meaning of a word by a prefix or suffix alone, you *can* use your knowledge of what root words mean to eliminate answer choices; indicating if the word is positive or negative can give you a partial meaning of the word.

PRACTICE DRILL – PREFIXES and SUFFIXES
What are the affixes in each word?

1. Disease
   a) Dis-
   b) -ise-
   c) -eas-
   d) -ase

2. Uncomfortable
   a) Un-
   b) Un-, -com-
   c) -fort-
   d) Un-, -able

3. Disrespected
   a) Re-, -spect, -ed
   b) Dis-, -ed
   c) Dis-, re-, -ed
   d) Respect-, -ed

4. Impressive
   a) Im-, -ive
   b) -ive
   c) Press-, -ive
   d) Impre-, -ive

5. Predated
   a) Pre-
   b) Pre-, -d
   c) Pre-, -ed
   d) –d

Using your knowledge of prefixes and root words, try to determine the meaning of the words in the following questions.

6. To take <u>precaution</u> is to:
   a) Prepare before doing something.
   b) Remember something that happened earlier.
   c) Become aware of something for the first time.
   d) Try to do something again.

7. To <u>reorder</u> a list is to:
   a) Use the same order again.
   b) Put the list in a new order.
   c) Get rid of the list.
   d) Find the list.

8. An <u>antidote</u> to a disease is:
   a) Something that is part of the disease.
   b) Something that works against the disease.
   c) Something that makes the disease worse.
   d) Something that has nothing to do with the disease.

9. Someone who is <u>multiethnic:</u>
   a) Likes only certain kinds of people.
   b) Lives in the land of his or her birth.
   c) Is from a different country.
   d) Has many different ethnicities.

10. Someone who is <u>misinformed</u> has been:
   a) Taught something new.
   b) Told the truth.
   c) Forgotten.
   d) Given incorrect information.

Choose the best answer to each question. (Remember you are looking for the closest meaning.)

11. <u>Exorbitant</u> means:
   a) Belonging to a group.
   b) To orbit.
   c) Beneath conscious awareness.
   d) Far beyond what is normal or reasonable.

12. <u>Denunciation</u> means:
   a) To denounce or openly condemn.
   b) Critical, of or like a condemnation.
   c) One who denounces or openly condemns another.
   d) The act of denouncing or openly condemning.

13. <u>Metamorphosis</u> means:
   a) To transform.
   b) One who has changed.
   c) A transformation.
   d) Tending to change frequently.

14. To <u>reconcile</u> means:
   a) To reestablish a close relationship between.
   b) To move away from.
   c) To undermine.
   d) To surpass or outdo.

15. <u>Didactic</u> means:
   a) A teacher or instructor.
   b) Intended to instruct, moralizing.
   c) To preach or moralize.
   d) The process of instructing.

16. <u>Unilateral</u> means:
   a) To multiply.
   b) Understated.
   c) Literal.
   d) One-sided.

17. <u>Subordinate</u> means:
   a) Under someone else's authority or control.
   b) Organized according to rank; hierarchical.
   c) Something ordinary or average, without distinction.
   d) Repeated frequently to aid memorization.

18. <u>Incisive</u> means:
   a) Insight.
   b) Worthy of consideration.
   c) Penetrating.
   d) To act forcefully.

19. <u>Intermittent</u> means:
   a) Badly handled.
   b) Occurring at intervals
   c) Greatly varied.
   d) A number between one and ten.

20. <u>Miscreant</u> means:

    a) Someone who is unconventional.

    b) Someone who lacks creativity.

    c) A very naive person.

    d) An evil person or villain.

ANSWERS – PREFIXES and SUFFIXES

1. **a) Dis-.** The prefix **dis-** means away from, deprive of, reversal, or not. If someone has a **disease** they are not well.

2. **d) Un-, -able.** The prefix **un-** means not. The suffix **-able** means ability or worthy of. **Uncomfortable** means not able to be in a state of comfort.

3. **c) Dis-, re-, -ed.** The prefix **dis-** means away from, reversal, or not. The prefix **re-** means back or again. The suffix **-ed** indicates that the word is in the past tense. **Disrespected** means showed a lack of respect towards.

4. **a) Im-, -ive.** The prefix **im-** means in, into, or within. The suffix **-ive** means having the nature of. **Impressive** means having the ability inspire an internal feeling of awe.

5. **c) Pre-, -ed.** The prefix **pre-** means before. The suffix **-ed** indicates that the word is in the past tense. **Predated** means came before the date.

6. **a) Prepare before doing something.** Pre- means before; to take **caution** is to be careful or take heed.

7. **b) Put the list in a new order.** *Re-* means again. In this case, order means organize. Reorder then means to organize the list again or to put the list into a different order.

8. **b) Something that works against the disease.** The prefix **anti-** means against. An **antidote** is something that works against a disease or a poison.

9. **d) Has many different ethnicities.** The prefix **multi-** means many. Someone who is **multiethnic** has relatives from many different ethnic groups.

10. **d) Given incorrect information.** Mis- means opposite, and to be **informed** is to have the correct information.

11. **d) Far beyond what is normal or reasonable.** The prefix **ex-** means out, out of, away from.

12. **a) The act of denouncing or openly condemning.** The prefix **de-** means against, the root **nounc** means to state or declare, and the noun suffix **-tion** means the act or state of.

13. **c) A transformation.** The prefix **meta-** means change, while the root **morph** means shape or form, and the **noun** suffix **-sis** means the process of. **Metamorphosis** means a marked change of form or a transformation.

14. a) Means to reestablish a relationship. The prefix **re-** means back or again and, the root **con** means with. Together they mean back together again or reestablishing a relationship.

15. b) Intended to instruct or moralize. The adjective suffix **-ic** means pertaining or relating to, having the quality of. Only choices **b** and **d** define a quality, and choice **d** would require an additional suffix.

16. d) One-sided. The prefix **uni-** means one.

17. a) Under someone else's authority or control. The prefix **sub-** means under, beneath or below.

18. c) Penetrating . The adjective suffix **-ive** means having the nature of.

19. b) Occurring at intervals. The prefix **inter-** means between or among.

20. d) An evil person or villain. The prefix **mis-** means bad, evil, or wrong. The suffix **–ant** means an agent or something that performs the action.

SYNONYMS and ANTONYMS

Synonyms are groups of words that mean the same, or almost the same, thing as each other. The word synonym comes from the Greek roots **syn-,** meaning same, and **-nym,** meaning name. **Hard, difficult, challenging,** and **arduous** are synonyms of one another.

Antonyms are sets of words that have opposite, or nearly opposite, meanings of one another. The word antonym comes from the Greek roots **ant-,** meaning opposing, and **–nym** (name). **Hard** and **easy** are antonyms.

Synonyms do not always have exactly the same meanings, and antonyms are not always exact opposites.. For example, scalding is an adjective that means burning. Boiling water can be described as scalding or as hot. **Hot** and **scalding** are considered synonyms, even though the two words do not mean exactly the same thing; something that is scalding is considered to be extremely hot.

In the same manner, antonyms are not always exact opposites. **Cold** and **freezing** are both antonyms of scalding. Although freezing is closer to being an exact opposite of scalding, cold is still considered an antonym. Antonyms can often be recognized by their prefixes and suffixes.

Here are rules that apply to prefixes and suffixes of antonyms:

- **Many antonyms can be created simply by adding prefixes.** Certain prefixes, such as *a-, de-, non-,* and *un-,* can be added to words to turn them into antonyms. **Atypical** is an antonym of **typical,** and **nonjudgmental** is an antonym of **judgmental.**

- **Some prefixes and suffixes are antonyms of one another.** The prefixes **ex-** (out of) and **in-/il-/im-/ir-** (into) are antonyms, and are demonstrated in the antonym pair **exhale/inhale.** Other prefix pairs that indicate antonyms include **pre-/post-, sub-/super-,** and **over-/under-.** The suffixes **-less,** meaning without, and **-ful,** meaning full of, often indicate that words are antonyms as well. For example: **meaningless** and **meaningful** are antonyms.

PRACTICE DRILL – SYNONYMS AND ANTONYMS
In each sentence or group of sentences, choose whether the underlined words are synonyms, antonyms, or neither.

1. I think Mrs. Robinson is <u>honest</u>, but Jordan thinks she's <u>treacherous.</u>

2. Marley is making a <u>stew</u> for the class potluck, while Tara is cooking a <u>roast</u>.

3. The doctors agreed that the disease was not <u>terminal</u>. This came as welcome news to the man's family, who feared it might be <u>life-threatening</u>.

4. My grandfather <u>built</u> his house on the side of a mountain. He <u>erected</u> the house with his own two hands in the 1960s.

5. I always assumed Lisa was <u>sociable</u>; at the dance, however, she seemed rather <u>bashful</u>.

6. Many animals prey on rabbits, so rabbits tend to move <u>cautiously</u>. Lions do not have any natural predators, so they walk very <u>boldly</u>.

7. Our basement was full of old <u>junk</u>, so we gathered up all the <u>trash</u> and put it in bags.

8. Most people in the class were <u>excited</u> to go on a field trip, but Janet was <u>unenthusiastic.</u>

9. Terrah likes <u>English</u> class the most, while Durrell prefers <u>Spanish</u>.

10. The villagers ran for <u>safety</u> during the <u>dangerous</u> storm.

Choose the best answer choice for the following questions.

11. <u>Awe</u> is most dissimilar to:

    a) Contempt.

    b) Reverence.

    c) Valor.

    d) Distortion.

12. <u>Intricate</u> is most similar to:

    a) Delicate.

    b) Costly.

    c) Prim.

    d) Complex.

13. <u>Skeptic</u> is most dissimilar to:

    a) Innovator.

    b) Friend.

    c) Politician.

    d) Believer.

14. <u>Hypothetical</u> is most dissimilar to:

    a) Uncritical.

    b) Actual.

    c) Specific.

    d) Imaginary.

15. <u>Enhance</u> is most dissimilar to:

    a) Diminish.

    b) Improve.

    c) Digress.

    d) Deprive.

16. <u>Manipulate</u> is most similar to:

    a) Simplify.

    b) Deplete.

    c) Nurture.

    d) Handle.

17. <u>Subjective</u> is most dissimilar to:

    a) Invective.

    b) Objectionable.

    c) Unbiased.

    d) Obedient.

18. <u>Succinct</u> is most dissimilar to:
   a) Distinct.
   b) Laconic.
   c) Feeble.
   d) Verbose.

19. <u>Enthusiastic</u> is most similar to:
   a) Adamant.
   b) Available.
   c) Cheerful.
   d) Eager.

20. <u>Adequate</u> is most similar to:
   a) Sufficient.
   b) Mediocre.
   c) Proficient.
   d) Average.

21. <u>Uniform</u> is most dissimilar to:
   a) Dissembling.
   b) Diverse.
   c) Bizarre.
   d) Slovenly.

22. <u>Ecstatic</u> is most similar to:
   a) Inconsistent.
   b) Positive.
   c) Wild.
   d) Thrilled.

ANSWERS – SYNONYMS AND ANTONYMS

1. **Antonyms.**

2. **Neither.**

3. **Synonyms.**

4. **Synonyms.**

5. **Antonyms.**

6. **Antonyms.**

7. **Synonyms.**

8. **Antonyms.**

9. **Neither.**

10. **Neither.**

11. **a) Contempt.** To be **awe** of something is to admire it; to have **contempt** for something is to consider it worthless.

12. **d) Complex.** Intricate means having many elaborately arranged elements; **complex** means complicated or involved.

13. **d) Believer.** A **skeptic** is someone who doubts; a **believer** is one who thinks something is true.

14. **b) Actual.** To be **hypothetical** is to be contingent on being tested; to be **actual** is to exist in fact.

15. **a) Diminish.** To **enhance** is to increase; to **diminish** is to decrease.

16. **d) Handle.** To **manipulate** is to manage or to **handle** in a governing manner.

17. **c) Unbiased.** To be **subjective** is to be influenced by one's own emotions or beliefs without regard to evidence presented; to be **unbiased** is to be objective or impartial.

18. **d) Verbose.** To be **succinct** is to be brief and to the point; to be **verbose** is to use excessive words, to be wordy.

19. **d) Eager.** Enthusiastic bother mean showing great earnestness.

20. **a) Sufficient.** If something is **adequate**, it is considered to be **sufficient**.

21. **b) Diverse.** To be **uniform** is to be consistent or the same as others; to be **diverse** is to have variety.

22. **d) Thrilled.** A person who is **ecstatic** is delighted or **thrilled**.

REVIEW

So far, you have learned that context clues are words within the sentence that help convey the meaning of the word you are looking for. There are two different kinds of context: sentence context and situational context.

Sentence context occurs immediately in the sentence surrounding the vocabulary word. The first thing you should do when looking for sentence context clues is determine the most significant words in the sentence and derive their meanings. Next, look at the answer choices and choose the one that makes the most sense in the sentence, considering those words.

Situational context is context that comes from understanding the situation in which a word or phrase occurs.

There are four types of clues:

Restatement clues are clues in which the word is openly defined.

Positive/negative clues tell you whether the word has a positive or negative meaning.

Contrast clues include the opposite meaning of a word.

Specific Detail clues give details about the word, though not its exact meaning.

These four types of clues are often used in combination.

Remember that roots are the basic unit of meaning in words. When you read a word that is unfamiliar to you, divide the word into syllables and look for the root by removing any prefixes and suffixes.

You have also learned that prefixes and suffixes are known collectively as **affixes**. Although affixes are not words by themselves, they are added to roots or words to change the meaning of roots or change a word's part of speech. **Prefixes** that change or enhance the meanings of words, and are found at the beginning of words. **Suffixes** change or enhance the meanings of words and/or change parts of speech and are found at the end of words.

You have also learned that **synonyms** are words that have the same or almost the same meaning, while **antonyms** are words that have opposite or nearly opposite meanings. Synonyms and antonyms of a word will always share the same part of speech. That is, a synonym or antonym of a verb has to be a verb; a synonym or antonym of an adjective has to be an adjective; and so forth. We also learned that not all words have synonyms or antonyms, and that synonyms do not always have exactly the same meaning, just as antonyms do not have to be exact opposites.

TIPS

- Look carefully at the context of the sentence itself to avoid bringing your own contextual meaning.

- Don't forget to pay attention to the connotation of all the important words in the sentence in addition to the question word.

- Look for introductory words and phrases, such as these: unfortunately, however, surprisingly, however, and on the other hand. These words have a strong influence on the question word's meaning.

- Remember to look for specific details that provide clues to meaning.

- Use words that you are very familiar with as examples when you study word roots. The more familiar the word is to you, the easier it will be for you to remember the meaning of the root word. Use words that create a vivid picture in your imagination.

- Be sure to look at all parts of the word as well as the context, if there is any, to determine meaning.

- Remember the power of elimination on an exam. Use your knowledge of word roots to eliminate incorrect answers. The more you narrow down your choices, the better your chances of choosing the correct answer.

- Roots do not always match the exact definitions of words. Another important thing to keep in mind is that sometimes one root will have several different spellings.

- Affixes do not have to be attached directly to a root. A word can often have more than one affix, even more than one prefix or suffix. For instance, the word **unremarkably** has two prefixes (un- and re-) and two suffixes (-able and -ly).

On the next few pages, you will find an extensive list of common roots and affixes.

Root or Affix	Meaning	Examples
a, ac, ad, af, ag, al, an, ap, as, at	To, toward, near, in addition to, by	Aside, accompany, adjust, aggression, allocate, annihilate, affix, associate, attend, adverb
a-, an-	Not, without	Apolitical, atheist, anarchy, anonymous, apathy
ab, abs	Away from, off	Absolve, abrupt, absent
-able, -ible	Adjective: worth, ability	Solvable, incredible
acer, acid, acri	Bitter, sour, sharp	Acerbic, acidity, acrid, acrimony
act, ag	Do, act, drive	Active, react, agent, active, agitate
Acu	Sharp	Acute, acupuncture, accurate
-acy, -cy	Noun: state or quality	Privacy, infancy, adequacy, intimacy, supremacy
-ade	Act, product, sweet drink	Blockade, lemonade
aer, aero	Air, atmosphere, aviation	Aerial, aerosol, aerodrome
ag, agi, ig, act	Do, move, go	Agent, agenda, agitate, navigate, ambiguous, action
-age	Noun: activity, or result of action	Courage, suffrage, shrinkage, tonnage
agri, agro	Pertaining to fields or soil	Agriculture, agroindustry
-al	Noun: action, result of action	Referral, disavowal, disposal, festival
-al, -ial, -ical	Adjective: quality, relation	Structural, territorial, categorical
alb, albo	White, without pigment	Albino, albeit
ali, allo, alter	Other	Alias, alibi, alien, alloy, alter, alter ego, altruism
alt	High, deep	Altimeter, altitude
am, ami, amor	Love, like, liking	Amorous, amiable, amicable, enamored
ambi	Both	Ambidextrous
ambul	To walk	Ambulatory, amble, ambulance, somnambulist
-an	Noun: person	Artisan, guardian, historian, magician

Root or Affix	Meaning	Examples
a, ano	Up, back, again, anew	Anode, anagram
nce, -ence	Noun: action, state, quality or process	Resistance, independence, extravagance, fraudulence
ncy, -ency	Noun: state, quality or capacity	Vacancy, agency, truancy, latency
dr, andro	Male, characteristics of men	Androcentric, android
g	Angular	Angle
im	Mind, life, spirit, anger	Animal, animate, animosity
n, annu, enni	Yearly	Annual, annual, annuity, anniversary, perennial
nt, -ent	Noun: an agent, something that performs the action	Disinfectant, dependent, fragrant
nt, -ent, -ient	Adjective: kind of agent, indication	Important, dependent, convenient
te	Before	Anterior, anteroom, antebellum, antedate, antecedent antediluvian
hrop	Man	Anthropology, misanthrope, philanthropy
i, ant	Against, opposite	Antisocial, antiseptic, antithesis, antibody, antinomies, antifreeze, antipathy
i, antico	Old	Antique, antiquated, antiquity
o, ap, aph	Away from, detached, formed	Apology, apocalypse
u	Water	Aqueous
, -ary	Adjective: resembling, related to	Spectacular, unitary
h	Chief, first, rule	Archangel, architect, archaic, monarchy, matriarchy, patriarchy
d, -art	Noun: characterized	Braggart, drunkard, wizard
er, astr	Star	Aster, asterisk, asteroid, astronomy, astronaut
e	Noun: state, office, function	Candidate, electorate, delegate

Root or Affix	Meaning	Examples
-ate	Verb: cause to be	Graduate, ameliorate, amputate, colligate
-ate	Adjective: kind of state	Inviolate
-ation	Noun: action, resulting state	Specialization, aggravation, alternation
auc, aug, aut	To originate, to increase	Augment , author, augment, auction
aud, audi, aur, aus	To hear, listen	Audience, audio, audible, auditorium, audiovisual, audition, auricular
aug, auc	Increase	Augur, augment, auction
aut, auto	Self	Automobile, automatic, automotive, autograph, autonomous, autoimmune
bar	Weight, pressure	Barometer
be	On, around, over, about, excessively, make, cause, name, affect	Berate, bedeck, bespeak, belittle, beleaguer
belli	War	Rebellion, belligerent, casus belli, bellicose
bene	Good, well, gentle	Benefactor, beneficial, benevolent, benediction, beneficiary, benefit
bi, bine	Two	Biped, bifurcate, biweekly, bivalve, biannual
bibl, bibli, biblio	Book	Bibliophile, bibliography, Bible
bio, bi	Life	Biography, biology biome, biosphere
brev	Short	Abbreviate, brevity, brief
cad, cap, cas, ceiv, cept, capt, cid, cip	To take, to seize, to hold	Receive, deceive, capable, capacious, captive, accident, capture, occasion, concept, intercept, forceps, except, reciprocate
cad, cas	To fall	Cadaver, cadence, cascade
-cade	Procession	Motorcade
calor	Heat	Calorie, caloric, calorimeter

Root or Affix	Meaning	Examples
ɔit, capt	Head	Decapitate, capital, captain, caption
n	Flesh	Carnivorous, incarnate, reincarnation, carnal
, cata, cath	Down, with	Catalogue, category, catheter
ıs, caut	Burn, heat	Caustic, cauldron, cauterize
ıse, cuse, cus	Cause, motive	Because, excuse, accusation
ıs, ced, cede, ɛd, cess	To go, to yield, move, go, surrender	Succeed, proceed, precede, recede, secession, exceed, succession
ıt	Hundred	Centennial, century, centipede
ıtr, centri	Center	Eccentricity, centrifugal, concentric, eccentric
ɔm	Color	Chrome, chromosome, polychrome, chromatic
ɔn	Time	Chronology, chronic, chronicle, synchronize
le, cis, cise	To kill, to cut, cut down	Homicide, incision, circumcision, scissors
cum	Around	Circumnavigate, circumflex, circumstance, circumference, circumvent, circulatory
	Call, start	Incite, citation, cite
	Citizen	Civic, civil, civilian, civilization
ɔt, claim	Cry out	Exclamation, clamor, proclamation, reclamation, acclaim
ı	Lean, bend	Decline, inclination
d, clus claus	To close, shut	Include, exclude, clause, claustrophobia, enclose, exclusive, reclusive, conclude
cog, col, coll, ı, com, cor	With, together	Cohesiveness, collaborate, convene, commitment, compress, contemporary, converge, compact, convenient, conjoin, combine, correct
ɡn, gnos	To know	Recognize, cognizant, diagnose, incognito, prognosis

Root or Affix	Meaning	Examples
com, con	Fully	Complete, compel, conscious, condense, confess, confirm
contr, contra, counter	Against, opposite	Contradict, counteract, contravene, contrary, counterspy, contrapuntal
cord, cor, cardi	Heart	Cordial, concord, discord, courage, encourage
corp	Body	Corporation, corporal punishment, corpse, corpulent
cort	Correct	Escort, cortege
cosm	Universe, world	Cosmos, microcosm, cosmopolitan, cosmonaut
cour, cur, curr, curs	Run, course	Occur, excursion, discourse, courier, course
crat, cracy	Rule	Autocrat, aristocrat, theocracy, technocracy
cre, cresc, cret, crease	Grow	Create, crescent, accretion, increase
crea	Create	Creature, recreation, creation
cred	Believe	Creed, credo, credence, credit, credulous, incredulous, incredible
cresc, cret, crease, cru	Rise, grow	Crescendo, concrete, increase, decrease, accrue
crit	Separate, choose	Critical, criterion, hypocrite
cur, curs	Run	Current, concurrent, concur, incur, recur, occur, courier, precursor, cursive
cura	Care	Curator, curative, manicure
cycl, cyclo	Wheel, circle, circular	Cyclops, unicycle, bicycle, cyclone, cyclic
de-	From, down, away, to do the opposite, reverse, against	Detach, deploy, derange, decrease, deodorize, devoid, deflate, degenerate
dec, deca	Ten, ten times	Decimal, decade, decimate, decathlon
dec, dign	Suitable	Decent decorate dignity

Root or Affix	Meaning	Examples
i, div	God	Divinity, divine, deity, divination, deify
m, demo	People, populace, population	Democracy, demography, demagogue, epidemic
nt, dont	Tooth	Dental, denture, orthodontist, periodontal
m	Skin, covering	Hypodermic, dermatology, epidermis, taxidermy
, dy-	Two, twice, double	Divide, diverge
i	Through, across, between	Diameter, diagonal, dialogue dialect, dialectic, diagnosis, diachronic
, dict, dit	Say, speak	Dictation, dictionary, dictate, dictator, Dictaphone, edict, predict, verdict, contradict, benediction
, dif	Not, opposite of, reverse, separate, deprive of, away	Dismiss, differ, disallow, disperse, dissuade, divide, disconnect, disproportion, disrespect, distemper, disarray
	Give	Credit, audit
c, doct	Teach, prove	Docile, doctor, doctrine, document, dogma, indoctrinate
min	Master, that which is under control	Dominate, dominion, predominant, domain
n	Give	Donate, condone
m	Sleep	Dormant, dormitory
x	Thought, opinion, praise	Orthodox, heterodox, paradox, doxology
ome	Run, step	Syndrome, aerodrome
c, duct	To lead, pull	Produce, abduct, product, transducer, viaduct, aqueduct, induct, deduct, reduce, induce
ra	Hard, lasting	Durable, duration, endure
nam	Power	Dynamo, dynamic, dynamite, hydrodynamics
s-	Bad, abnormal, difficult, impaired, unfavorable	Dysfunctional, dyslexia

Root or Affix	Meaning	Examples
e-	Not, missing, out, fully, away, computer network related	Emit, embed, eternal, ether, erase, email
ec-	Out of, outside	Echo, eclipse, eclectic, ecstasy
eco-	Household, environment, relating to ecology or economy	Ecology, economize, ecospheres
ecto-	Outside, external	Ectomorph, ectoderm, ectoplasm
-ed	Verb: past tense	Dressed, faded, patted, closed, introduced
-ed	Adjective: having the quality or characteristics of	Winged, moneyed, dogged, tiered
-en	Verb: to cause to become	Lengthen, moisten, sharpen
-en	Adjective: material	Golden, woolen, silken
en-, em-	Put into, make, provide with, surround with	Enamor, embolden, enslave, empower, entangle
-ence, -ency	Noun: action or process, quality or state	Reference, emergency, dependence, eminence, latency
end-	Inside, within	Endorse, endergonic, endoskeleton, endoscope,
epi-	Upon, close to, over, after, altered	Epicenter, epilogue, epigone
equi-	Equal	Equidistant, equilateral, equilibrium, equinox, equation, equator
-er, -ier	Adjective: comparative	Better, brighter, sooner, hotter, happier
-er, -or	Noun: person or thing that does something	Flyer, reporter, player, member, fryer, collector, concentrator
-er, -or	Verb: action	Ponder, dishonor, clamor
erg	Work, effect	Energy, erg, allergy, ergometer
-ery	Collective qualities, art, practice, trade, collection, state, condition	Snobbery, bakery, greenery, gallery, slavery

Root or Affix	Meaning	Examples
es, -ies	Noun: plural of most nouns ending in -ch, -s, -sh, -o and -z and some in -f and -y	Passes, glasses, ladies, heroes
es, -ies	Verb: third person singular present indicative of verbs that end in -ch, -s, -sh, - and some in -y	Blesses, hushes, fizzes, defies
ess	Female	Actress, goddess, poetess
est, -iest	Adjective or Adverb: superlative	Latest, strongest, luckiest
v-, et-	Time, age	Medieval, eternal
x-	Out of, away from, lacking, former	Exit, exhale, exclusive, exceed, explosion, ex-mayor
xter-, extra-, xtro-	Outside of, beyond	External, extrinsic, extraordinary, extrapolate, extraneous, extrovert
a, fess	Speak	Fable, fabulous, fame, famous, confess, profess
ac, fact, fec, fect, ic, fas, fea	Do, make	Difficult, fashion, feasible, feature, factory, effect, manufacture, amplification, confection
all, fals	Deceive	Fallacy, falsify, fallacious
emto	Quadrillionth	Femtosecond
er	Bear, carry	Ferry, coniferous, fertile, defer, infer, refer, transfer
c, feign, fain, fit, eat	Shape, make, fashion	Fiction, faint, feign
d	Belief, faith	Confide, diffident, fidelity
d, fide, feder	Faith, trust	Confidante, fidelity, confident, infidelity, infidel, federal, confederacy,
g	Shape, form	Effigy, figure, figment
la, fili	Thread	Filigree, filament, filter, filet, filibuster
n	End, ended, finished	Final, finite, finish, confine, fine, refine, define, finale

Root or Affix	Meaning	Examples
fix	Repair, attach	Fix, fixation, fixture, affix, prefix, suffix
flex, flect	Bend	Flex, reflex, flexible, flexor, inflexibility, reflect, deflect, circumflex
flict	Strike	Affliction, conflict, inflict
flu, fluc, fluv, flux	Flow	Influence, fluid, flue, flush, fluently, fluctuate, reflux, influx
-fold	Adverb: in a manner of, marked by	Fourfold
for, fore	Before	Forecast, fortune, foresee
forc, fort	Strength, strong	Effort, fort, forte, fortifiable, fortify, forte, fortitude
form	Shape, resemble	Form, format, conform, formulate, perform, formal, formula
fract, frag, frai	Break	Fracture, infraction, fragile, fraction, refract, frail
fuge	Flee	Subterfuge, refuge, centrifuge
-ful	Noun: an amount or quantity that fills	Mouthful
-ful	Adjective: having, giving, marked by	Fanciful
fuse	Pour	Confuse, transfuse
-fy	Make, form into	Falsify, dandify
gam	Marriage	Bigamy, monogamy, polygamy
gastr, gastro	Stomach	Gastric, gastronomic, gastritis, gastropod
gen	Kind	Generous
gen	Birth, race, produce	Genesis, genetics, eugenics, genealogy, generate, genetic, antigen, pathogen
geo	Earth	Geometry, geography, geocentric, geology

Root or Affix	Meaning	Examples
germ	Vital part	Germination, germ, germane
gest	Carry, bear	Congest, gestation
giga	Billion	Gigabyte, gigaflop
gin	Careful	Gingerly
gloss, glot	Tongue	Glossary, polyglot, epiglottis
glu, glo	Lump, bond, glue	Glue, agglutinate, conglomerate
gor	To gather, to bring together	Category, categorize
grad, gress, gree	To gather, to bring together, step, go	Grade, degree, progress, gradual, graduate, egress
graph, gram, graf	Write, written, draw	Graph, graphic, autograph, photography, graphite, telegram, polygraph, grammar, biography, lithograph, graphic
grat	Pleasing	Congratulate, gratuity, grateful, ingrate
grav	Heavy, weighty	Grave, gravity, aggravate, gravitate
greg	Herd	Gregarious, congregation, segregate
hale, heal	Make whole, sound	Inhale, exhale, heal, healthy, healthiness
helio	Sun	Heliograph, heliotrope, heliocentric
hema, hemo	Blood	Hemorrhage, hemoglobin, hemophilia, hemostat
her, here, hes	Stick	Adhere, cohere, cohesion, inherent, hereditary, hesitate
hetero	Other, different	Heterodox, heterogeneous, heterosexual, heterodyne
hex, ses, sex	Six	Hexagon, hexameter, sestet, sextuplets
homo	Same	Homogenize, homosexual, homonym, homophone
hum, human	Earth, ground, man	Humus, exhume, humane

Root or Affix	Meaning	Examples
hydr, hydra, hydro	Water	Dehydrate, hydrant, hydraulic, hydraulics, hydrogen, hydrophobia
hyper	Over, above	Hyperactive, hypertensive, hyperbolic, hypersensitive, hyperventilate, hyperkinetic
hypn	Sleep	Hypnosis, hypnotherapy
-ia	Noun: names, diseases	Phobia
-ian, an	Noun: related to, one that is	Pedestrian, human
-iatry	Noun: art of healing	Psychiatry
-ic	Adjective: quality, relation	Generic
-ic, ics	Noun: related to the arts and sciences	Arithmetic, economics
-ice	Noun: act	Malice
-ify	Verb: cause	Specify
ignis	Fire	Ignite, igneous, ignition
-ile	Adjective: having the qualities of	Projectile
in, im	Into, on, near, towards	Instead, import
in, im, il, ir	Not	Illegible, irresolute, inaction, inviolate, innocuous, intractable, innocent, impregnable, impossible, imposter
infra	Beneath	Infrared, infrastructure
-ing	Noun: material made for, activity, result of an activity	Flooring, swimming, building
-ing	Verb: present participle	Depicting
-ing	Adjective: activity	Cohering
inter	Between, among	International, intercept, interject, intermission, internal, intermittent

Root or Affix	Meaning	Examples
ra	Within, during, between layers, underneath	Intramural, intranet
ro	Into, within, inward	Interoffice, introvert, introspection, introduce
n	Noun: condition or action	Abduction
n	Adjective: having the character of	Newish
n	Noun: doctrine, belief, action or conduct	Formalism
	Noun: person or member	Podiatrist
t	Noun: state or quality	Graphite
y, ty	Noun: state or quality	Lucidity, novelty
e	Noun: condition	Native
e, -ative, -itive	Adjective: having the quality of	Festive, cooperative, sensitive
e	Verb: cause	Fantasize
, ject	Throw	Reject, eject, project, trajectory, interject, dejected, inject, ejaculate, adjacent
n, junct	Join	Adjoining, enjoin, juncture, conjunction, injunction, conjunction
ice	Judge	Prejudice
, junct, just	To join	Junction, adjust, conjugal
en	Young	Juvenile, rejuvenate
or	Work	Laborious, belabor
, lav, lot, lut	Wash	Launder, lavatory, lotion, ablution, dilute
, leg, lig	Choose, gather, select, read	Collect, legible, eligible
	Law	Legal, legislate, legislature, legitimize

Root or Affix	Meaning	Examples
-less	Adjective: without, missing	Motiveless
levi	Light	Alleviate, levitate, levity
lex, leag, leg	Law	Legal, college, league
liber, liver	Free	Liberty, liberal, liberalize, deliverance
lide	Strike	Collide, nuclide
liter	Letters	Literary, literature, literal, alliteration, obliterate
loc, loco	Place, area	Location, locally, locality, allocate, locomotion
log, logo, ology	Word, study, say, speech, reason, study	Catalog, prologue, dialogue, zoology, logo
loqu, locut	Talk, speak	Eloquent, loquacious, colloquial, circumlocution
luc, lum, lun, lus, lust	Light	Translucent, luminary, luster, lunar, illuminate, illustrate
lude	Play	Prelude
-ly	Adverb: in the manner of	Fluently
macr-, macer	Lean	Emaciated, meager
magn	Great	Magnify, magnificent, magnanimous, magnate, magnitude, magnum
main	Strength, foremost	Mainstream, mainsail, domain, remain
mal	Bad, badly	Malformation, maladjusted, dismal, malady, malcontent, malfunction, malfeasance, maleficent
man, manu	Hand, make, do	Manual, manage, manufacture, manacle, manicure, manifest, maneuver, emancipate, management
mand	Command	Mandatory, remand, mandate
mania	Madness	Mania, maniac, kleptomania, pyromania
mar, mari, mer	Sea, pool	Marine, marsh, maritime, mermaid

Root or Affix	Meaning	Examples
tri	Mother	Matrimony, maternal, matriarchate, matron
di	Half, middle, between, halfway	Mediate, medieval, Mediterranean, mediocre
ga	Great, million	Megaphone, megaton, megabyte, megalopolis
m	Recall, remember	Memo, commemoration, memento, memoir, memorable
nt	Mind	Mental, mention
ent	Noun: condition or result	Document
so	Middle	Mesomorph, mesosphere
ta	Beyond, change	Metaphor, metamorphosis, metabolism,
ter	Measure	Meter, voltammeter, barometer, thermometer
tr	Admeasure, apportion	Metrics, asymmetric, parametric, telemetry
cro	Small, millionth	Microscope, microfilm, microwave, micrometer
gra	Wander	Migrate, emigrant, immigrate
l, kilo	Thousand	Millennium, kilobyte, kiloton
li	Thousandth	Millisecond, milligram, millivolt
n	Little, small	Minute, minor, minuscule
	Wrong, bad, badly	Misconduct, misinterpret, misnomer, mistake
, miss	Send	Emit, remit, submit, admit, commit, permit, transmit, omit, intermittent, mission, missile
b, mov, mot	Move	Motion, remove, mobile, motor
n	Warn, remind	Monument, admonition, monitor, premonition
no	One	Monopoly, monotype, monologue, mononucleosis
r, mort	Mortal, death	Mortal, immortal, mortality, mortician, mortuary

Root or Affix	Meaning	Examples
morph	Shape, form	Amorphous, dimorphic, metamorphosis, morphology, polymorphic, morpheme, amorphous
multi	Many, much	Multifold, multilingual, multiply, multitude, multipurpose, multinational
nano	Billionth	Nanosecond
nasc, nat, gnant, nai	To be born	Nascent, native, pregnant, naive
nat, nasc	To be from, to spring forth	Innate, natal, native, renaissance
neo	New	Neolithic, neologism, neophyte, neonate
-ness	Noun: state, condition, quality	Kindness
neur	Nerve	Neuritis, neuropathic, neurologist, neural, neurotic
nom	Law, order	Autonomy, astronomy, gastronomy, economy
nom, nym	Name	Nominate, synonym
nomen, nomin	Name	Nomenclature, nominate, ignominious
non	Nine	Nonagon
non	Not	Nonferrous, nonsense, nonabrasive, nondescript
nov	New	Novel, renovate, novice, nova, innovate
nox, noc	Night	Nocturnal, equinox
numer	Number	Numeral, numeration, enumerate, innumerable
numisma	Coin	Numismatics
nunci, nunc, nounc	Speak, declare, warn	Pronounce, announcement
ob, oc, of, op	Toward, against, in the way	Oppose, occur, offer, obtain
oct	Eight	Octopus, octagon, octogenarian, octave
oligo	Few, little	Oligocene, oligosaccharide, oligotrophic, oligarchy
omni	All, every	Omnipotent, omniscient, omnipresent, omnivorous

Root or Affix	Meaning	Examples
...ym	Name	Anonymous, pseudonym, antonym, synonym
...er	Work	Operate, cooperate, opus
	Noun: condition or activity	Valor, honor, humor, minor
...ho	Straight, correct	Orthodox, orthodontist, orthopedic, unorthodox
...y	Noun: place for, serves for	Territory, rectory
...us, -eous, -ose, -us	Adjective: having the quality of, relating to	Adventurous, courageous, verbose, fractious
...er	Excessive, above	Overwork, overall, overwork
...	Peace	Pacifist, pacify, pacific ocean
...r, pare	Arrange, assemblage, two	Repair, impair, compare, prepare
...eo	Old	Paleozoic, Paleolithic,
...n	All	Pan-American, pan-African, panacea, pandemonium
...ra	Beside	Paradox, paraprofessional, paramedic, paraphrase, parachute
..., pass, path	Feel, suffer	Patient, passion, sympathy, pathology
...er, patr	Father	Paternity, patriarch, patriot, patron, patronize
...h, pathy	Feeling, suffering	Pathos, sympathy, antipathy, apathy, telepathy
...d, pod	Foot	Pedal, impede, pedestrian, centipede, tripod,
...do	Child	Orthopedic, pedagogue, pediatrics
..., puls	Drive, push, urge	Compel, dispel, expel, repel, propel, pulse, impulse, pulsate, compulsory, expulsion, repulsive
...d, pens, pond	Hang, weigh	Pendant, pendulum, suspend, appendage, pensive, append
	Through, intensive	Persecute, permit, perspire, perforate, persuade

Root or Affix	Meaning	Examples
peri	Around	Periscope, perimeter, perigee, periodontal
phage	Eat	Macrophage, bacteriophage
phan, phas, phen, fan, phant, fant	Show, make visible	Phantom, fantasy
phe	Speak	Blaspheme, cipher, phenomenon, philosopher
phil	Love	Philosopher, philanthropy, philharmonic, bibliophile
phlegma	Inflammation	Phlegm, phlegmatic
phobia, phobos	Fear	Phobia, claustrophobia, homophobia
phon	Sound	Telephone, phonics, phonograph, phonetic, homophone, microphone, symphony, euphonious
phot, photo	Light	Photograph, photoelectric, photogenic, photosynthesis, photon
pict	Paint, show, draw	Picture, depict
plac, plais	Please	Placid, placebo, placate, complacent
pli, ply	Fold	Reply, implicate, ply
plore	Cry out, wail	Implore, exploration, deploring
plu, plur, plus	More	Plural, pluralist, plus
pneuma, pneumon	Breath	Pneumatic, pneumonia,
pod	Foot, feet	Podiatry, tripod
poli	City	Metropolis, police, politics, Indianapolis, megalopolis, acropolis
poly	Many	Polytheist, polygon, polygamy, polymorphous
pon, pos, pound	Place, put	Postpone, component, opponent, proponent, expose, impose, deposit, posture, position, expound, impound

Root or Affix	Meaning	Examples
pop	People	Population, populous, popular
port	Carry	Porter, portable, transport, report, export, import, support, transportation
portion	Part, share	Portion, proportion
post	After, behind	Postpone, postdate
pot	Power	Potential, potentate, impotent
pre, pur	Before	Precede
prehendere	Seize, grasp	Apprehend, comprehend, comprehensive, prehensile
prin, prim, prime	First	Primacy, primitive, primary, primal, primeval, prince, principal
pro	For, forward	Propel
proto	First	Prototype, protocol, protagonist, protozoan
psych	Mind, soul	Psyche, psychiatry, psychology, psychosis
punct	Point, dot	Punctual, punctuation, puncture, acupuncture
pute	Think	Dispute, computer
quat, quad	Four	Quadrangle, quadruplets
quint, penta	Five	Quintet, quintuplets, pentagon, pentane, pentameter
quip	Ship	Equip, equipment
quir, quis, quest, quer	Seek, ask	Query, inquire, exquisite, quest
re	Back, again	Report, realign, retract, revise, regain
reg, recti	Straighten	Regiment, regular, rectify, correct, direct, rectangle
retro	Backwards	Retrorocket, retrospect, retrogression, retroactive
ri, ridi, risi	Laughter	Deride, ridicule, ridiculous, derision, risible

Root or Affix	Meaning	Examples
rog, roga	Ask	Prerogative, interrogation, derogatory
rupt	Break	Rupture, interrupt, abrupt, disrupt
sacr, sanc, secr	Sacred	Sacred, sacrosanct, sanction, consecrate, desecrate
salv, salu	Safe, healthy	Salvation, salvage, salutation
sanct	Holy	Sanctify, sanctuary, sanction, sanctimonious, sacrosanct
sat, satis	Enough	Saturate, satisfy
sci, scio, scientia	Know	Science, conscious, omniscient
scope	See, watch	Telescope, microscope, kaleidoscope, periscope, stethoscope
scrib, script	Write	Scribe, scribble, inscribe, describe, subscribe, prescribe, manuscript
se	Apart, move away from	Secede
sect, sec	Cut	Intersect, transect, dissect, secant, section
sed, sess, sid	Sit	Sediment, session, obsession, possess, preside, president, reside, subside
semi	Half, partial	Semifinal, semiconscious, semiannual, semimonthly, semicircle
sen, scen	Old, grow old	Senior, senator, senile, senescence, evanescent
sent, sens	Feel, think	Sentiment, consent, resent, dissent, sentimental, sense, sensation, sensitive, sensory, dissension
sept	Seven	Septet, septennial
sequ, secu, sue	Follow	Sequence, consequence, sequel, subsequent, prosecute, consecutive, second, ensue, pursue
serv	Save, serve, keep	Servant, service, subservient, servitude, preserve, conserve, reservation, deserve, conservation, observe
-ship	Noun: status, condition	Relationship, friendship

Root or Affix	Meaning	Examples
sign, signi	Sign, mark, seal	Signal, signature, design, insignia, significant
simil, simul	Like, resembling	Similar, assimilate, simulate, simulacrum, simultaneous
sist, sta, stit	Stand, withstand, make up	Assist, insist, persist, circumstance, stamina, status, state, static, stable, stationary, substitute
soci	To join, companions	Sociable, society
sol, solus	Alone	Solo, soliloquy, solitaire, solitude, solitary, isolate
solv, solu, solut	Loosen, explain	Solvent, solve, absolve, resolve, soluble, solution, resolution, resolute, dissolute, absolution
somn	Sleep	Insomnia, somnambulist
soph	Wise	Philosophy, sophisticated
spec, spect, spi, spic	Look, see	Specimen, specific, spectator, spectacle, aspect, speculate, inspect, respect, prospect, retrospective, introspective, expect, conspicuous
sper	Render favorable	Prosper
sphere	Ball, sphere	Sphere, stratosphere, hemisphere, spheroid
spir	Breath	Spirit, conspire, inspire, aspire, expire, perspire, respiration
stand, stant, stab, stat, stan, sti, sta, stead	Stand	Stature, establish, stance
-ster	Person	Mobster, monster
strain, strict, string, stige	Bind, pull, draw tight	Stringent, strict, restrict, constrict, restrain, boa constrictor
stru, struct, stroy, stry	Build	Construe, structure, construct, instruct, obstruct, destruction, destroy, industry, ministry
sub, suc, suf, sup, sur, sus	Under, below, from, secretly, instead of	Sustain, survive, support, suffice, succeed, submerge, submarine, substandard, subvert
sume, sump	Take, use, waste	Consume, assume, sump, presumption

Root or Affix	Meaning	Examples
super, supra	Over, above	Superior, suprarenal, superscript, supernatural, superimpose
syn, sym	Together, at the same time	Sympathy, synthesis, synchronous, syndicate
tact, tang, tag, tig, ting	Touch	Tactile, contact, intact, intangible, tangible, contagious, contiguous, contingent
tain, ten, tent, tin	Hold, keep, have	Retain, continue, content, tenacious
tect, teg	Cover	Detect, protect, tegument
tele	Distance, far, from afar	Telephone, telegraph, telegram, telescope, television, telephoto, telecast, telepathy, telepathy
tem, tempo	Time	Tempo, temporary, extemporaneously, contemporary, pro tem, temporal
ten, tin, tain	Hold	Tenacious, tenant, tenure, untenable, detention, retentive, content, pertinent, continent, obstinate, contain, abstain, pertain, detain
tend, tent, tens	Stretch, strain	Tendency, extend, intend, contend, pretend, superintend, tender, extent, tension, pretense
tera	Trillion	Terabyte, teraflop
term	End, boundary, limit	Exterminate, terminal
terr, terra	Earth	Terrain, terrarium, territory, terrestrial
test	To bear witness	Testament, detest, testimony, attest, testify
the, theo	God, a god	Monotheism, polytheism, atheism, theology
therm	Heat	Thermometer, theorem, thermal, thermos bottle, thermostat, hypothermia
thesis, thet	Place, put	Antithesis, hypothesis, synthesis, epithet
tire	Draw, pull	Attire, retire, entire
tom	Cut	Atom (not cutable), appendectomy, tonsillectomy, dichotomy, anatomy

Root or Affix	Meaning	Examples
tor, tors, tort	Twist	Torture, retort, extort, distort, contort, torsion, tortuous, torturous
tox	Poison	Toxic, intoxicate, antitoxin
tract, tra, trai, treat	Drag, draw, pull	Attract, tractor, traction, extract, retract, protract, detract, subtract, contract, intractable
trans	Across, beyond, change	Transform, transoceanic, transmit, transportation, transducer
tri	Three	Tripod, triangle, trinity, trilateral
trib	Pay, bestow	Tribute, contribute, attribute, retribution, tributary
tribute	Give	Contribute, distribute, tributary
turbo	Disturb	Turbulent, disturb, turbid, turmoil
typ	Print	Type, prototype, typical, typography, typewriter, typology, typify
ultima	Last	Ultimate, ultimatum
umber, umbraticum	Shadow	Umbra, penumbra, (take) umbrage, adumbrate
un	Not, against, opposite	Unceasing, unequal
uni	One	Uniform, unilateral, universal, unity, unanimous, unite, unison, unicorn
-ure	Noun: act, condition, process, function	Exposure, conjecture, measure
vac	Empty	Vacate, vacuum, evacuate, vacation, vacant, vacuous
vade	Go	Evade, invader
vale, vali, valu	Strength, worth	Equivalent, valiant, validity, evaluate, value, valor
veh, vect	To carry	Vector, vehicle, convection, vehement
ven, vent	Come	Convene, intervene, venue, convenient, avenue, circumvent, invent, convent, venture, event, advent, prevent

Root or Affix	Meaning	Examples
ver, veri	True	Very, aver, verdict, verity, verify, verisimilitude
verb, verv	Word	Verify, veracity, verbalize, verve
vert, vers	Turn, change	Convert, revert, advertise, versatile, vertigo, invert, reversion, extravert, introvert, diversion, introvert, convertible, reverse, controversy
vi	Way	Viable, vibrate, vibrant
vic, vicis	Change, substitute	Vicarious, vicar, vicissitude
vict, vinc	Conquer	Victor, evict, convict, convince, invincible
vid, vis	See	Video, evident, provide, providence, visible, revise, supervise, vista, visit, vision, review, indivisible
viv, vita, vivi	Alive, life	Revive, survive, vivid, vivacious, vitality, vital, vitamins, revitalize
voc, voke	Call	Vocation, avocation, convocation, invocation, evoke, provoke, revoke, advocate, provocative, vocal
vol	Will	Malevolent, benevolent, volunteer, volition
volcan	Fire	Volcano, vulcanize, Vulcan
volv, volt, vol	Turn-about, roll	Revolve, voluble, voluminous, convolution, revolt, evolution
vor	Eat greedily	Voracious, carnivorous, herbivorous, omnivorous, devour
-ward	Adverb: in a direction or manner	Homeward
-wise	Adverb: in the manner of, with regard to	Clockwise, bitwise
with	Against	Withhold, without, withdraw, forthwith
-y	Noun: state, condition, result of an activity	Society, victory
-y	Adjective: marked by, having	Hungry, angry, smeary, teary

Root or Affix	Meaning	Examples
	Animal	Zoo (zoological garden), zoology, zodiac, protozoan

Chapter 2: Paragraph Comprehension

The Paragraph Comprehension test measures your ability to understand, analyze, and evaluate written passages. The passages will contain material from a variety of sources and on a number of different topics, and consists of 15 multiple choice questions to be answered in 13 minutes. This chapter of the book will discuss the various types of questions typically asked.

The Main Idea

Finding and understanding the main idea of a text is an essential reading skill. When you look past the facts and information and get to the heart of what the writer is trying to say, that's the **main idea**.

Imagine that you're at a friend's home for the evening:
> "Here," he says, "Let's watch this movie."
> "Sure," you reply. "What's it about?"

You'd like to know a little about what you'll be watching, but your question may not get you a satisfactory answer, because you've only asked about the subject of the film. The subject—what the movie is about—is only half the story. Think, for example, about all the alien invasion films ever been made. While these films may share the same general subject, what they have to say about the aliens or about humanity's theoretical response to invasion may be very different. Each film has different ideas it wants to convey about a subject, just as writers write because they have something they want to say about a particular subject. When you look beyond the facts and information to what the writer really wants to say about his or her subject, you're looking for the main idea.

One of the most common questions on reading comprehension exams is, "What is the main idea of this passage?" How would you answer this question for the paragraph below?

> "Wilma Rudolph, the crippled child who became an Olympic running champion, is an inspiration for us all. Born prematurely in 1940, Wilma spent her childhood battling illness, including measles, scarlet fever, chicken pox, pneumonia, and polio, a crippling disease which at that time had no cure. At the age of four, she was told she would never walk again. But Wilma and her family refused to give up. After years of special treatment and physical therapy, 12-year-old Wilma was able to walk normally again. But walking wasn't enough for Wilma, who was determined to be an athlete. Before long, her talent earned her a spot in the 1956 Olympics, where she earned a bronze medal. In the 1960 Olympics, the height of her career, she won three gold medals."

What is the main idea of this paragraph? You might be tempted to answer, "Wilma Rudolph" or "Wilma Rudolph's life." Yes, Wilma Rudolph's life is the **subject** of the passage—who or what the passage is about—but the subject is not necessarily the main idea. The **main idea** is what the writer wants to say about this subject. What is the main thing the writer says about Wilma's life?

Which of the following statements is the main idea of the paragraph?

a) Wilma Rudolph was very sick as a child.
b) Wilma Rudolph was an Olympic champion.
c) Wilma Rudolph is someone to admire.

Main idea: The overall fact, feeling, or thought a writer wants to convey about his or her subject.

The best answer is **c**): Wilma Rudolph is someone to admire. This is the idea the paragraph adds up to; it's what holds all of the information in the paragraph together. This example also shows two important characteristics of a main idea:

1. It is **general** enough to encompass all of the ideas in the passage.

2. It is an **assertion.** An assertion is a statement made by the writer.

The main idea of a passage must be general enough to encompass all of the ideas in the passage. It should be broad enough for all of the other sentences in that passage to fit underneath it, like people under an umbrella. Notice that the first two options, "Wilma Rudolph was very sick as a child" and "Wilma Rudolph was an Olympic champion", are too specific to be the main idea. They aren't broad enough to cover all of the ideas in the passage, because the passage talks about both her illnesses and her Olympic achievements. Only the third answer is general enough to be the main idea of the paragraph.

A main idea is also some kind of **assertion** about the subject. An assertion is a claim that something is true. Assertions can be facts or opinions, but in either case, an assertion should be supported by specific ideas, facts, and details. In other words, the main idea makes a general assertion that tells readers that something is true. The supporting sentences, on the other hand, show readers that this assertion is true by providing specific facts and details. For example, in the Wilma Rudolph paragraph, the writer makes a general assertion: "Wilma Rudolph, the crippled child who became an Olympic running champion, is an inspiration for us all." The other sentences offer specific facts and details that prove why Wilma Rudolph is an inspirational person.

Writers often state their main ideas in one or two sentences so that readers can have a very clear understanding about the main point of the passage. A sentence that expresses the main idea of a paragraph is called a **topic sentence.**

Notice, for example, how the first sentence in the Wilma Rudolph paragraph states the main idea:

"Wilma Rudolph, the crippled child who became an Olympic running champion, is an inspiration for us all."

This sentence is therefore the topic sentence for the paragraph. Topic sentences are often found at the beginning of paragraphs. Sometimes, though, writers begin with specific supporting ideas and lead up to the main idea, and in this case the topic sentence is often found at the end of the paragraph. Sometimes the topic sentence is even found somewhere in the middle, and other times there isn't a clear topic sentence at all—but that doesn't mean there isn't a main idea; the author has just chosen not to express it in a clear topic sentence. In this last case, you'll have to look carefully at the paragraph for clues about the main idea.

Main Ideas vs. Supporting Ideas

If you're not sure whether something is a main idea or a supporting idea, ask yourself the following question: is the sentence making a **general statement,** or is it providing **specific information?** In the Wilma Rudolph paragraph above, for example, all of the sentences except the first make specific statements. They are not general enough to serve as an umbrella or net for the whole paragraph.

Writers often provide clues that can help you distinguish between main ideas and their supporting ideas. Here are some of the most common words and phrases used to introduce specific examples:

1. **For example...**
2. **Specifically...**
3. **In addition...**
4. **Furthermore...**
5. **For instance...**
6. **Others...**
7. **In particular...**
8. **Some...**

These signal words tell you that a supporting fact or idea will follow. If you're having trouble finding the main idea of a paragraph, try eliminating sentences that begin with these phrases, because they will most likely be too specific to be a main ideas.

Implied Main Idea

When the main idea is implied, there's no topic sentence, which means that finding the main idea requires some detective work. But don't worry! You already know the importance of structure, word choice, style, and tone. Plus, you know how to read carefully to find clues, and you know that these clues will help you figure out the main idea.

For Example:

> "One of my summer reading books was *The Windows of Time*. Though it's more than 100 pages long, I read it in one afternoon. I couldn't wait to see what happened to Evelyn, the main character. But by the time I got to the end, I wondered if I should have spent my afternoon doing something else. The ending was so awful that I completely forgot that I'd enjoyed most of the book."

There's no topic sentence here, but you should still be able to find the main idea. Look carefully at what the writer says and how she says it. What is she suggesting?

a) *The Windows of Time* is a terrific novel.
b) *The Windows of Time* is disappointing.
c) *The Windows of Time* is full of suspense.
d) *The Windows of Time* is a lousy novel.

The correct answer is **b)** – the novel is disappointing. How can you tell that this is the main idea? First, we can eliminate choice **c)**, because it's too specific to be a main idea. It deals only with one specific aspect of the novel (its suspense).

Sentences **a)**, **b)**, and **d)**, on the other hand, all express a larger idea – a general assertion about the quality of the novel. But only one of these statements can actually serve as a "net" for the whole paragraph. Notice that while the first few sentences praise the novel, the last two criticize it. Clearly, this is a mixed review.

Therefore, the best answer is **b)**. Sentence **a)** is too positive and doesn't account for the "awful" ending. Sentence **d)**, on the other hand, is too negative and doesn't account for the reader's sense of suspense and interest in the main character. But sentence **b)** allows for both positive and negative aspects – when a good thing turns bad, we often feel disappointed.

Now let's look at another example. Here, the word choice will be more important, so read carefully.

> "Fortunately, none of Toby's friends had ever seen the apartment where Toby lived with his mother and sister. Sandwiched between two burnt-out buildings, his two-story apartment building was by far the ugliest one on the block. It was a real eyesore: peeling orange paint (orange!), broken windows, crooked steps, crooked everything. He could just imagine what his friends would say if they ever saw this poor excuse for a building."

Which of the following expresses the main idea of this paragraph?

> a)   Toby wishes he could move to a nicer building.
> b)   Toby wishes his dad still lived with them.
> c)   Toby is glad none of his friends know where he lives.
> d)   Toby is sad because he doesn't have any friends.

From the description, we can safely assume that Toby doesn't like his apartment building and wishes he could move to a nicer building **a)**. But that idea isn't general enough to cover the whole paragraph, because it's about his building.

Because the first sentence states that Toby has friends, the answer cannot be **d)**. We know that Toby lives only with his mother and little sister, so we might assume that he wishes his dad still lived with them, **b)**, but there's nothing in the paragraph to support that assumption, and this idea doesn't include the two main topics of the paragraph—Toby's building and Toby's friends.

What the paragraph adds up to is that Toby is terribly embarrassed about his building, and he's glad that none of his friends have seen it **c)**. This is the main idea. The paragraph opens with the word "fortunately," so we know that he thinks it's a good thing none of his friends have been to his house. Plus, notice how the building is described: "by far the ugliest on the block," which says a lot since it's stuck "between two burnt-out buildings." The writer calls it an "eyesore," and repeats "orange" with an exclamation point to emphasize how ugly the color is. Everything is "crooked" in this "poor excuse for a building." Toby is clearly ashamed of where he lives and worries about what his friends would think if they saw it.

Context Clues

Often in your reading you will come across words or phrases that are unfamiliar to you. How can you understand what you're reading if you don't know what all the words mean? You can often use **context** to determine meaning! That is, by looking carefully at the sentences and ideas surrounding an unfamiliar word, you can often figure out exactly what that word means.

For example, read the following paragraph:

> "Andy is the most unreasonable, pigheaded, subhuman life-form in the entire galaxy, and he makes me so angry I could scream! Of course, I love him like a brother. I sort of have to, because he *is* my brother. More than that, he's my twin! That's right. Andy and Amy (that's me) have the same curly hair and dark eyes. Yet though we look alike, we have

very different dispositions. You could say that we're opposites. While I'm often quiet and pensive, Andy is loud and doesn't seem to stop to think about anything. Oh, and did I mention that he's the most stubborn person on the planet?"

As you read this passage, you probably came across at least two unfamiliar words: **dispositions** and **pensive**. While a dictionary would be helpful, you don't need to look up these words. The paragraph provides enough clues to help you figure out what these words mean.

Let's begin with **dispositions**. In what context is this word used? Let's take another look at the sentence in which it's used and the two sentences that follow: "Yet though we look alike, we have very different dispositions. You could say that we're opposites. While I'm often quiet and **pensive**, Andy is loud and doesn't seem to stop to think about anything."

The context here offers several important clues:
1. The sentence in which **dispositions** is used tells us something about what dispositions are not.

2. The sentence sets up a contrast between the ways that Amy and Andy look and between their dispositions; this means that dispositions are not something physical.

3. The general content of the paragraph. We can tell from the paragraph that dispositions have something to do with who Andy and Amy are, since the paragraph describes their personalities.

4. Yet another clue is what follows the sentence in which **dispositions** is used. Amy offers two specific examples of their dispositions: She's quiet and pensive, while Andy is loud and doesn't seem to think much.

These are specific examples of personality traits. By now you should have a pretty good idea of what the word dispositions means. A disposition is:

a) A person's physical characteristics.
b) A person's preferences.
c) A person's natural qualities or tendencies.

The best answer, of course, is **c)**, a person's natural qualities or tendencies. While a person's disposition often helps determine his or her preferences, **b)**, this passage doesn't say anything about what Amy and Andy like to do (or not do). Nor are these characteristics physical, **a)**. Amy is talking about their personalities.

Now, let's look at the second vocabulary word: **pensive**. Again, the context provides us with strong clues. Amy states that she and Andy "are opposites"—that though they look alike, they have opposite dispositions; she is quiet, and he is loud. So we can expect that the next pair of descriptions will be opposites, too.

Now we simply have to look at her description of Andy and come up with its opposite. If Andy "doesn't seem to stop to think about anything," then we can assume that Amy spends a lot of time thinking.

We can therefore conclude that *pensive* means:

    a) Intelligent, wise.
    b) Deep in thought.
    c) Considerate of others.

The best answer is **b)**, deep in thought. If you spend a lot of time thinking, that may make you wise. But remember, we're looking for the opposite of Andy's characteristics, so neither **a)** nor **c)** can be the correct answer.

When you're trying to determine meaning from context on an exam, two strategies can help you find the best answer.

1. First, determine whether the vocabulary word is something positive or negative. If the word is something positive, then eliminate the answers that are negative, and vice versa.

2. Replace the vocabulary word with the remaining answers, one at a time. Does the answer make sense when you read the sentence? If not, you can eliminate that answer.

Cause and Effect

Understanding cause and effect is important for reading success. Every event has at least one cause (what made it happen) and at least one effect (the result of what happened). Some events have more than one cause, and some have more than one effect. An event is also often part of a chain of causes and effects. Causes and effects are usually signaled by important transitional words and phrases.

Words Indicating Cause:
    1. Because (of)
    2. Created (by)
    3. Caused (by)
    4. Since

Words Indicating Effect:
    1. As a result
    2. Since
    3. Consequently
    4. So
    5. Hence
    6. Therefore

Sometimes, a writer will offer his or her opinion about why an event happened when the facts of the cause(s) aren't clear. Or a writer may predict what he or she thinks will happen because of a certain event (its effects). If this is the case, you need to consider how reasonable those opinions are. Are the writer's ideas logical? Does the writer offer support for the conclusions he or she offers?

Reading Between the Lines

Paying attention to word choice is particularly important when the main idea of a passage isn't clear. A writer's word choice doesn't just affect meaning; it also creates it. For example, look at the following description from a teacher's evaluation of a student applying to a special foreign language summer camp. There's no topic sentence, but if you use your powers of observation, you should be able to tell how the writer feels about her subject.

> "As a student, Jane usually completes her work on time and checks it carefully. She speaks French well and is learning to speak with less of an American accent. She has often been a big help to other students who are just beginning to learn the language."

What message does this passage send about Jane? Is she the best French student the writer has ever had? Is she one of the worst, or is she just average? To answer these questions, you have to make an inference, and you must support your inference with specific observations. What makes you come to the conclusion that you come to?

The **diction** of the paragraph above reveals that this is a positive evaluation, but not a glowing recommendation.

Here are some of the specific observations you might have made to support this conclusion:

1. The writer uses the word "usually" in the first sentence. This means that Jane is good about meeting deadlines for work, but not great; she doesn't always hand in her work on time.

2. The first sentence also says that Jane checks her work carefully. While Jane may sometimes hand in work late, at least she always makes sure it's quality work. She's not sloppy.

3. The second sentence tells us she's "learning to speak with less of an American accent." This suggests that she has a strong accent and needs to improve in this area. It also suggests, though, that she is already making progress.

4. The third sentence tells us that she "often" helps "students who are just beginning to learn the language." From this we can conclude that Jane has indeed mastered the basics. Otherwise, how could she be a big help to students who are just starting to learn? By looking at the passage carefully, then, you can see how the writer feels about her subject.

PRACTICE DRILL – PARAGRAPH COMPREHENSION
Read each of the following paragraphs carefully and answer the questions that follow.

My "office" measures a whopping 5 x 7 feet. A large desk is squeezed into one corner, leaving just enough room for a rickety chair between the desk and the wall. Yellow paint is peeling off the walls in dirty chunks. The ceiling is barely six feet tall; it's like a hat that I wear all day long. The window, a single 2 x 2 pane, looks out onto a solid brick wall just two feet away.

1. What is the main idea implied by this paragraph?
   a) This office is small but comfortable.
   b) This office is in need of repair.
   c) This office is old and claustrophobic.
   d) None of the above.

There are many things you can do to make tax time easier. The single most important strategy is to keep accurate records. Keep all of your pay stubs, receipts, bank statements, and other relevant financial information in a neat, organized folder so that when you're ready to prepare your form, all of your paperwork is in one place. The second thing you can do is start early. Get your tax forms from the post office as soon as they are available and start calculating. This way, if you run into any problems, you have plenty of time to straighten them out. You can also save time by reading the directions carefully. This will prevent time-consuming errors. Finally, if your taxes are relatively simple (you don't have itemized deductions or special investments), use the shorter tax form. It's only one page, so if your records are in order, it can be completed in less than an hour.

2. How many suggestions for tax time does this passage offer?
   a) One.
   b) Two.
   c) Three.
   d) Four.

3. The sentence "It's only one page, so if your records are in order, it can be completed in less than an hour" is:
   a) The main idea of the passage.
   b) A major supporting idea.
   c) A minor supporting idea.
   d) A transitional sentence.

4. A good summary of this passage would be:
   a) Simple strategies can make tax time less taxing.
   b) Don't procrastinate at tax time.
   c) Always keep good records.
   d) Get a tax attorney.

5. According to the passage, who should use the shorter tax form?
   a) Everybody.
   b) People who do not have complicated finances.
   c) People who do have complicated finances.
   d) People who wait until the last minute to file taxes.

6. The sentence, "The single most important strategy is to keep accurate records," is a(n):
   a) Fact.
   b) Opinion.
   c) Both of the above.
   d) Neither of the above.

Being a secretary is a lot like being a parent. After a while, your boss becomes dependent upon you, just as a child is dependent upon his or her parents. Like a child who must ask permission before going out, you'll find your boss coming to you for permission, too. "Can I have a meeting on Tuesday at 3:30?" you might be asked, because you're the one who keeps track of your boss's schedule. You will also find yourself cleaning up after your boss a lot, tidying up papers and files the same way a parent tucks away a child's toys and clothes. And, like a parent protects his or her children from outside dangers, you will find yourself protecting your boss from certain "dangers"—unwanted callers, angry clients, and upset subordinates.

7. The main idea of this passage is:
   a) Secretaries are treated like children.
   b) Bosses treat their secretaries like children.
   c) Secretaries and parents have similar roles.
   d) Bosses depend too much upon their secretaries.

8. Which of the following is the topic sentence of the paragraph?
   a) Being a secretary is a lot like being a parent.
   b) After a while, your boss becomes dependent upon you, just as a child is dependent upon his or her parents.
   c) You will also find yourself cleaning up after your boss a lot, tidying up papers and files the same way a parent tucks away a child's toys and clothes.
   d) None of the above.

9. According to the passage, secretaries are like parents in which of the following ways?
   a) They make their bosses' lives possible.
   b) They keep their bosses from things that might harm or bother them.
   c) They're always cleaning and scrubbing things.
   d) They don't get enough respect.

10. This passage uses which point of view?
   a) First person.
   b) Second person.
   c) Third person.
   d) First and second person.

11. The tone of this passage suggests that:
   a) The writer is angry about how secretaries are treated.
   b) The writer thinks secretaries do too much work.
   c) The writer is slightly amused by how similar the roles of secretaries and parents are.
   d) The writer is both a secretary and a parent.

12. The sentence, "'Can't I have a meeting on Tuesday at 3:30?' you might be asked, because you're the one who keeps track of your boss's schedule," is a:
   a) Main idea.
   b) Major supporting idea.
   c) Minor supporting idea
   d) None of the above.

13. "Being a secretary is a lot like being a parent" is:
   a) A fact.
   b) An opinion.
   c) Neither of the above.
   d) Both of the above.

14. The word "subordinates" probably means:
   a) Employees.
   b) Parents.
   c) Clients.
   d) Secretaries.

Day after day, Johnny chooses to sit at his computer instead of going outside with his friends. A few months ago, he'd get half a dozen phone calls from his friends every night. Now, he might get one or two a week. It used to be that his friends would come over two or three days a week after school. Now, he spends his afternoons alone with his computer.

15. The main idea is:
   a) Johnny and his friends are all spending time with their computers instead of one another.
   b) Johnny's friends aren't very good friends.
   c) Johnny has alienated his friends by spending so much time on the computer.
   d) Johnny and his friends prefer to communicate by computer.

We've had Ginger since I was two years old. Every morning, she wakes me up by licking my cheek. That's her way of telling me she's hungry. When she wants attention, she'll weave in and out of my legs and meow until I pick her up and hold her. And I can always tell when Ginger wants to play. She'll bring me her toys and will keep dropping them (usually right on my homework!) until I stop what I'm doing and play with her for a while.

16. A good topic sentence for this paragraph would be:
   a) I take excellent care of Ginger.
   b) Ginger is a demanding pet.
   c) Ginger and I have grown up together.
   d) Ginger is good at telling me what she wants.

ANSWERS – PARAGRAPH COMPREHENSION

1. c)
2. d)
3. c)
4. a)
5. b)
6. b)
7. c)
8. a)
9. b)
10. b)
11. c)
12. c)
13. b)
14. a)
15. c)
16. d)

Chapter 3: Arithmetic Reasoning

The Arithmetic reasoning tests your ability to use fundamental math concepts to solve word problems. During the test, you will have 30 minutes to answer 36 problems. The most important step in solving any word problem is to read the entire problem before beginning to solve. You shouldn't skip over words or assume you know what the question is from the first sentence. The following are the general steps used to solve word problems:

General Steps for Word Problem Solving:

Step 1: Read the entire problem and determine what the problem is asking for.

Step 2: List all of the given data.

Step 3: Sketch diagrams with the given data.

Step 4: Determine formula(s) needed.

Step 5: Set up equation(s).

Step 6: Solve.

Step 7: Check your answer. Make sure that your answer makes sense. (Is the amount too large or small; are the answers in the correct unit of measure; etc.)

Note: Not all steps are needed for every problem.

In chapter four, you will be given a list of the most commonly-made mistakes on the mathematics knowledge test – they will apply here as well. Even if an answer you calculated is a given answer choice, that doesn't make it the correct answer. Remember that not all of the information given in a problem is needed to solve it.

For example:
Kathy had $12.45, John had $10.30, and Liz had $6.90. How much money did the girls have combined?

The amount John has is not needed to solve the problem, since the problem is only asking for the combined amounts of Kathy and Liz.

Mistakes most commonly occur when answers for only a part of the problem are given as answer choices. It's very easy to get caught up in thinking, "That's the number I have here! It looks right, so I'll go with that." Trust yourself, and always check your answers. The best way to prepare for the arithmetic section is to practice! At first, don't concern yourself with how long it takes to solve problems; focus on understanding how to solve them, and then time yourself. (For the complete list of commonly-made mistakes, go to page 115.)

This section will go over some of the most common types of word problems found on the Arithmetic Reasoning Section, but keep in mind that any math concept can be turned into a word problem.

Key Words

Word problems generally contain key words that can help you determine what math processes may be required in order to solve them. Here are some commonly-used key words:

- **Addition:** Added, combined, increased by, in all, total, perimeter, sum, and more than.
- **Subtraction:** How much more, less than, fewer than, exceeds, difference, and decreased.
- **Multiplication:** Of, times, area, and product.
- **Division:** Distribute, share, average, per, out of, percent, and quotient.
- **Equals:** Is, was, are, amounts to, and were.

BASIC WORD PROBLEMS

A word problem in algebra is the equivalent of a story problem in math, only word problems are solved by separating information from the problems into two equal groups (one for each side of an equation). Examine this problem:

> Sara has 15 apples and 12 oranges. How many pieces of fruit does she have?

We know that the sum of 15 and 12 is equal to the total amount of fruit. An unknown number or value is represented by a letter. The total number of pieces of fruit is unknown, so we will represent that amount with x. When the value that a particular variable will represent is determined, it is defined by writing a statement like this:

> Let x = Total Amount of Fruit

Once again, the sum of 15 apples and 12 oranges is equal to the total amount of fruit. This can be used to translate the problem into an equation:

> $15 + 12 = x$
> $x = 27$
> Sara has 27 pieces of fruit.

Of course, you could probably have solved this problem more quickly without having set up an algebraic equation. But knowing how to use an equation for this kind of problem builds your awareness of which concepts are useful; some of them are even critical to solving much harder problems.

Examples:

1. A salesman bought a case of 48 backpacks for $576. He sold 17 of them for $18 at the swap meet, and the rest were sold to a department store for $25 each. What was the salesman's profit?

    Calculate the total of the 17 backpacks, which you know the cost to be $18:
    $17 * \$18 = \$306$

    Calculate how many backpacks were sold at $25:
    $48 - 17 = 31$

    Calculate the total amount of profit for the backpacks sold at $25:
    $31 \times \$25 = \$775$

    Add the two dollar amounts for backpacks sold:
    $\$306 + \$775 = \$1081$

    Subtract the salesman's initial cost:
    $\$1081 - \$576 = \$505$

    The answer to the question asked about his profit is: $505.

2. Thirty students in Mr. Joyce's room are working on projects over the duration of two days. The first day, he gave them 3/5 of an hour to work. On the second day, he gave them half as much time as the first day. How much time did the students have altogether?

1st day = 3/5 of an hour
2nd day = 1/2 (3/5) = 3/10 of an hour
Total = 3/5 + 3/10 = 6/10 + 3/10 = 9/10 of an hour

An hour has 60 minutes, so set up a ratio:

9/10 = x/60
x = 54
So the students had 54 minutes altogether to work on the projects.

Another way to do this problem is to calculate first the amount of time allotted on the first day:

3/5 * 60 minutes = 36 minutes

Then take half of that to get the time allotted on the second day:

36 minutes * 1/2 = 18 minutes

Add the two together for your total time!

36 + 18 = 54

CONSECUTIVE NUMBER PROBLEMS

Examples:

1. Two consecutive numbers have a sum of 91. What are the numbers?

To begin solving this problem, define the variable. You do not know what the first consecutive number is, so you can call it x.

The First Consecutive Number = x

Since the numbers are consecutive, meaning one number comes right after the other, the second number must be one more than the first. So, $x + 1$ equals the second number.

The Second Consecutive Number = $x + 1$

The problem states that the sum of the two numbers is 91. This can be shown in the equation like the following:

$x + (x + 1) = 91$

That equation can be solved as follows:

Initial Equation: $x + (x + 1) = 91$

Combine Like Terms: $2x + 1 = 91$

After subtracting 1 from each side: $2x = 90$

After dividing each side by 2, $x = 45$

Careful! In a situation like this, it's almost a sure thing that one of the answer choices will be "45" on the test. This is a trap! You aren't done with your problem yet. Remember, x only equals the value of the first consecutive number – you want the sum of *both*.

Since x equals 45, and the Second Consecutive Number equals $x + 1$, you can simply add 1 to 45 to find that Second Consecutive Number. It should be shown like the work below:

Let x = The First Consecutive Number = 45
Let $x + 1$ = The Second Consecutive Number = 46

$$x + (x + 1) \quad = \quad 91$$

Don't forget to check your work!

$$2x + 1 = 91$$

$$2x = 90$$

$$x = 45$$

Sometimes you will encounter a problem which has more than two consecutive numbers, such as:

1. When added, four consecutive numbers have a sum of 18. What is the largest number?

> You can solve this much like the previous problem. The difference is that you will have to define four numbers (instead of two).
>
> *Note*: Each consecutive number is found by adding 1 to the previous number.
>
> The First Consecutive Number = x
>
> The Second Consecutive Number = $x + 1$
>
> The Third Consecutive Number = $x + 2$
> The Fourth Consecutive Number = $x + 3$
>
> Your equation will look like this:
>
> $x + (x + 1) + (x + 2) + (x + 3) = 18$
>
> $4x + 6 = 18$
>
> $4x = 12$
>
> $x = 3$
>
> Remember the problem asked for largest number, x represents the smallest; so you aren't done!
>
> $x + 3 = 3$
> $3 + 3 = 6$

Even or Odd Consecutive Numbers

The only difference between ordinary consecutive numbers and even or odd consecutive numbers is the space between each number. Each consecutive number would add 2 instead of 1. The trick here is to remember that your first consecutive number will determine whether or not the following consecutive numbers will be even or odd. If the problem calls for even consecutive numbers, then your first number must be even; if odd, then the first number must be odd.

Many problems lend themselves to being solved with systems of linear equations.

1. The admission fee at a small fair is $1.50 for children and $4.00 for adults. On a certain day, 2,200 people enter the fair, and $5,050 is collected. How many children and how many adults attended?

Using a system of equations allows the use of two different variables for the two different unknowns.

Number of adults: a
Number of children: c

Total number: $a + c = 2200$
Total income: $4a + 1.5c = 5050$

Now solve the system for the number of adults and the number of children. Solve the first equation for one of the variables, and then substitute the result into the other equation.

Because $a + c = 2200$, we know that:

$a = 2200 - c$
$4(2200 - c) + 1.5c = 5050$
$8800 - 4c + 1.5c = 5050$
$8800 - 2.5c = 5050$
$-2.5c = -3750$
$c = 1500$

Now go back to that first equation.

$a = 2200 - (1500) = 700$

There were 1500 children and 700 adults

2. A landscaping company placed two orders with a nursery. The first order was for 13 bushes and 4 trees, and totaled $487. The second order was for 6 bushes and 2 trees, and totaled $232. The bills do not list the per-item price. What were the costs of one bush and of one tree?

First pick variables ("b" for the price of bushes and "t" for the price of trees) and set up a system of equations:

first order: $13b + 4t = 487$
second order: $6b + 2t = 232$

<u>Multiply</u> the second row by 2, so when they are subtracted, one variable is eliminated

<u>To subtract, multiple the second row by negative 1. Then you have:</u>

$13b + 4t = 487$
$-12b - 4t = -464$

This says that $b = 23$. Back-solving, you will find that $t = 47$.

Bushes cost $23 each; trees cost $47 each.

PERCENTAGE WORD PROBLEMS

Basic Equations:

Percent Change:
> Amount of Change ÷ Original Amount x 100

Percent Increase:
> (New Amount – Original Amount) ÷ Original Amount x 100

Percent Decrease:
> (Original Amount – New Amount) ÷ Original Amount x 100

Amount Increase (Or Amount Decrease):
> Original Price * Percent Markup (Or, for Amount Decrease, Markdown)

Original Price:
> New Price ÷ (Whole - Percent Markdown)

Original Price:
> New Price ÷ (Whole + Percent Markup)

Many percentage problems consist of markup and markdown. For these, you calculate how much the quantity changed, and then you calculate the percent change relative to the original value.

Examples:

1. A computer software retailer used a markup rate of 40%. Find the selling price of a computer game that cost the retailer $25.

    The markup is 40% of the $25 cost, so the equation to find markup is:

    (0.40) * (25) = 10

    The selling price is the cost plus markup:

    25 + 10 = 35

    The item sold for $35.

2. A golf shop pays its wholesaler $40 for a certain club, and then sells it to a golfer for $75. What is the markup rate?

First calculate the markup:

$$75 - 40 = 35$$

Then find the markup rate: $35 is (some percent) of $40, or:

$$35 = (x) * (40)$$

...so the markup over the original price is:

$$35 \div 40 = x$$
$$x = 0.875$$

Since the problem asks for a percentage, you need to remember to convert this decimal value to the corresponding percentage.

The markup rate is 87.5%.

3. A shoe store uses a 40% markup on cost. Find the cost of a pair of shoes that sells for $63.

This problem is somewhat backwards. You are given the selling price, which is "cost + markup", and the markup rate. You are not given the actual cost or markup.

Let x be the cost. The markup, being 40% of the cost, is $0.40x$. The selling price of $63 is the sum of the cost and markup, so:

$$63 = x + 0.40x$$
$$63 = 1x + 0.40x$$
$$63 = 1.40x$$
$$63 \div 1.40 = x$$
$$x = 45$$

The shoes cost the store $45.

4. An item originally priced at $55 is marked 25% off. What is the sale price?

First, find the markdown. The markdown is 25% of the original price of $55, so:

$x = (0.25) * (55)$
$x = 13.75$

By subtracting this markdown from the original price, you can find the sale price:

$55 - 13.75 = 41.25$

The sale price is $41.25.

5. An item that regularly sells for $425 is marked down to $318.75. What is the discount rate?

First, find the amount of the markdown:

$425 - 318.75 = 106.25$

Then calculate "the markdown of the original price", or the markdown rate:

$106.25 is (some percent) of $425, so:

$106.25 = (x) * (425)$

...and the markdown over the original price is:

$x = 106.25 \div 425$
$x = 0.25$

Since the "x" stands for a percentage, remember to convert this decimal to percentage form.

The markdown rate is 25%.

6. A bike is marked down 15%; the sale price is $127.46. What was the original price?

This problem is backwards. You are given the sale price ($127.46) and the markdown rate (15%), but neither the markdown amount nor the original price.

Let "x" stand for the original price. Then the markdown, being 15% of this price, will be 0.15x. The sale price is the original price, minus the markdown, so:

$$x - 0.15x = 127.46$$
$$1x - 0.15x = 127.46$$
$$0.85x = 127.46$$
$$x = 127.46 \div 0.85$$
$$x = 149.95$$

The original price was $149.95.

Note: In this last problem, I ended up – in the third line of calculations – with an equation that said "eighty-five percent of the original price is $127.46". You can save yourself some time if you think of discounts in this way: if the price is 15% off, then you're only actually paying 85%. Similarly, if the price is 25% off, then you're paying 75%, etc.

Note: While the values below do not refer to money, the procedures used to solve these problems are otherwise identical to the markup - markdown examples.

7. Growing up, you lived in a tiny country village. When you left for college, the population was 840. You recently heard that the population has grown by 5%. What is the present population?

First, find the actual amount of the increase. Since the increase is five percent of the original population, then the increase is:

$$(0.05) * (840) = 42$$

The new population is the old population plus the increase, or:

$$840 + 42 = 882$$

The population is now 882.

8. You put in an 18 × 51 foot garden along the whole back end of your backyard. It has reduced the backyard lawn area by 24%. What is the area of the remaining lawn area?

The area of the garden is:

$$(18) * (51) = 918$$

This represents 24% of the total yard area, or 24% of the original lawn area. This means that 918 square feet is 24% of the original, so:

$$918 = 0.24x$$
$$918 \div 0.24 = x$$
$$3825 = x$$

The total back yard area is 3825 square feet, and we know from the problem that the width is 51 feet. Therefore, to find the length:

$$3825 \div 51 = 75$$

The length then is 75 feet. Since 18 feet are taken up by the garden, then the lawn area is

$$75 - 18 = 57 \text{ feet deep.}$$

The area of the lawn now measures 51' × 57'

WORK WORD PROBLEMS

"Work" problems involve situations such as: two people working together to paint a house. You are usually told how long each person takes to paint a similarly-sized house, and then you are asked how long it will take the two of them to paint the house when they work together.

There is a "trick" to doing work problems: you have to think of the problem in terms of how much each person/machine/whatever does in a given unit of time.

For example:

Suppose one painter can paint the entire house in twelve hours, and the second painter takes eight hours. How long would it take the two painters together to paint the house?

If the first painter can do the entire job in twelve hours, and the second painter can do it in eight hours, then (here is the trick!) the first painter can do 1/12 of the job per hour, and the second guy can do 1/8 per hour. How much then can they do per hour if they work together?

To find out how much they can do together per hour, add together what they can do individually per hour: 1/12 + 1/8 = 5/24. They can do 5/24 of the job per hour.

Now let "t" stand for how long they take to do the job together. Then they can do 1/t per hour, so 5/24 = 1/t. When for t = 24/5, t = 4.8 hours. That is:

Hours to complete job:

First painter: 12
Second painter: 8
Together: t

Work completed per hour:

First painter: 1/12
Second painter: 1/8
Together: 1/t

Adding their labor:

1/12 + 1/8 = 1/t
5/24 = 1/t
24/5 = t
t = 4 4/5 hours

As you can see in the above example, "work" problems commonly create rational equations. But the equations themselves are usually pretty simple.

More Examples:

1. One pipe can fill a pool 1.25 times faster than a second pipe. When both pipes are opened, they fill the pool in five hours. How long would it take to fill the pool if only the slower pipe is used?

> Convert to rates:
>
> > Hours to complete job:
> > Fast pipe: f
> > Slow pipe: $1.25f$
> > Together: 5
> >
> > Work completed per hour:
> > Fast pipe: $1/f$
> > Slow pipe: $1/1.25f$
> > Together: $1/5$
> >
> > Adding their labor:
> > $1/f + 1/1.25f = 1/5$
> >
> > Solve for f:
> > $5 + 5/1.25 = f$
> > $5 + 4 = f$
> > $f = 9$
> > Then $1.25f = 11.25$, so the slower pipe takes 11.25 hours.
>
> If you're not sure how I derived the rate for the slow pipe, think about it this way: if someone goes twice as fast as you, then you take twice as long as he does; if he goes three times as fast, then you take three times as long. In this case, one pipe goes 1.25 times as fast, so the other takes 1.25 times as long.

This next one is a bit different:

2. Ben takes 2 hours to wash 500 dishes, and Frank takes 3 hours to wash 450 dishes. How long will they take, working together, to wash 1000 dishes?

> For this exercise, you are given *how many* can be done in one time unit, rather than *how much* of a job can be completed. But the thinking process is otherwise the same.
>
> Ben can do 250 dishes per hour, and Frank can do 150 dishes per hour. Working together, they can do $250 + 150 = 400$ dishes an hour. That is:
>
> > Ben: 500 dishes / 2 hours = 250 dishes / hour
> > Frank: 450 dishes / 3 hours = 150 dishes / hour
> > together: $(250 + 150)$ dishes / hour = 400 dishes / hour

Next find the number of hours that it takes to wash 1000 dishes. Set things up so <u>units cancel</u> and you're left with "hours:"

(1000 dishes) * (1 hour / 400 dishes)
(1000 / 400) hours
2.5 hours

It will take two and a half hours for the two of them to wash 1000 dishes.

3. If six men can do a job in fourteen days, how many would it take to do the job in twenty-one days?

Convert this to man-hours, or, in this case, man-days. If it takes six guys fourteen days, then:

(6 men) * (14 days) = 84 man-days

That is, the entire job requires 84 man-days. This exercise asks you to expand the time allowed from fourteen days to twenty-one days. Obviously, if they're giving you more time, then you'll need fewer guys. But how many guys, exactly?

(x men) * (21 days) = 84 man-days

...or, in algebra:

$21x = 84$

$x = 4$

So, only four guys are needed to do the job in twenty-one days.

You may have noticed that each of these problems used some form of the "how much can be done per time unit" construction, but aside from that each problem was done differently. That's how "work" problems are; but, as you saw above, if you label things neatly and do your work orderly, you should find your way to the solution.

DISTANCE WORD PROBLEMS

"Distance" word problems, often also called "uniform rate" problems, involve something travelling at a fixed and steady ("uniform") pace ("rate" or "speed"), or else moving at some average speed. Whenever you read a problem that involves "how fast", "how far, or "for how long," you should think of the distance equation, $d = rt$, where d stands for distance, r stands for the (constant or average) rate of speed, and t stands for time. It is easier to solve these types of problems using a grid and filling in the information given in the problem.

Warning: Make sure that the units for time and distance agree with the units for the rate. For instance, if they give you a rate of feet per second, then your time must be in seconds and your distance must be in feet. Sometimes they try to trick you by using two different units, and you have to catch this and convert to the correct units.

1. An executive drove from his home at an average speed of 30 mph to an airport where a helicopter was waiting. The executive boarded the helicopter and flew to the corporate offices at an average speed of 60 mph. The entire distance was 150 miles; the entire trip took three hours. Find the distance from the airport to the corporate offices.

	d	r	t
driving	d	30	t
flying	$150 - d$	60	$3 - t$
total	150	---	3

The first row gives me the equation $d = 30t$.

Since the first part of his trip accounted for d miles of the total 150-mile distance and t hours of the total 3-hour time, you are left with $150 - d$ miles and $3 - t$ hours for the second part. The second row gives the equation:

$$150 - d$$
$$d = 60(3 - t)$$

This now becomes a system of equations problem.

Add the two "distance" expressions and setting their sum equal to the given total distance:

$$150 - d = 60(3 - t)$$
$$d = 30t$$
$$150 = 30t + 60(3 - t)$$

Solve for t:

$$150 = 30t + 180 - 60t$$
$$150 = 180 - 30t$$
$$-30 = -30t$$
$$1 = t$$

It is important to note that you are not finished when you have solved for the first variable. This is where it is important to pay attention to what the problem asked for. It does not ask for time, but the time is needed to solve the problem.

So now insert the value for t into the first equation:
$$d = 30$$

Subtract from total distance:
$$150 - 30 = 120$$

The distance to the corporate offices is 120 miles.

2. Two cyclists start at the same time from opposite ends of a course that is 45 miles long. One cyclist is riding at 14 mph and the second cyclist is riding at 16 mph. How long after they begin will they meet?

	d	r	t
slow guy	d	14	t
fast guy	$45 - d$	16	t
total	45	---	---

Why is t the same for both cyclists? Because you are measuring from the time they both started to the time they meet somewhere in the middle.

Why "d" and "$45 - d$" for the distances? Because I assigned the slower cyclist as having covered d miles, which left $45 - d$ miles for the faster cyclist to cover: the two cyclists *together* covered the whole 45 miles.

Using "$d = rt$," you get $d = 14t$ from the first row, and $45 - d = 16t$ from the second row. Since these distances add up to 45, add the distance expressions and set equal to the given total:

$$45 = 14t + 16t$$

Solve for t, place it back into the equation, to solve for what the question asked.

$$45 = 30t \quad t = 45 \div 30 = 1\ 1/2$$

They will meet 1 ½ hours after they begin.

SIMPLE INTEREST

Formula for simple interest:

$I = PRT$

> I represents the interest earned.
>
> P represents the principal which is the number of dollars invested.
>
> T represents the time the money is invested; generally stated in years or fractions of a year.
>
> R represents the rate at which the principal (p) is earned.

Formula for Amount:

$A = P + I$

> A represents what your investment is worth if you consider the total amount of the original investment (P) and the interest earned (I).

Example:

If I deposit $500 in an account with an annual rate of 5%, how much will I have after 2 years?

1st yr: $500 + (500 * .05) = $525.

2nd yr: $525 + (525 * .05) = $ 551.25.

RATIO PROBLEMS

To solve a ratio, simply find the equivalent fraction. To distribute a whole across a ratio:

1. Total all parts.

2. Divide the whole by the total number of parts.

3. Multiply quotient by corresponding part of ratio.

Example:

There are 81 voters in a room, all either Democrat or Republican. The ratio of Democrats to Republicans is 5:4. How many republicans are there?

Step 1 $5 + 4 = 9$

Step 2 $81 \div 9 = 9$

Step 3 $9 * 4 = 36$

36 Republicans

Proportions
- **Direct proportions** – corresponding ratio parts change in the same direction (increase/decrease).

- **Indirect proportions** – corresponding ratio parts change in opposite directions; as one part increases the other decreases.

Example (Indirect Proportion):

A train traveling 120 miles takes 3 hours to get to its destination. How long will it take if the train travels 180 miles?

120 miles : 180 miles
is to
x hours : 3 hours

Write as a fraction and cross multiply:

$3 * 120 = 180x$
$360 = 180x$
$x = 2$ hours

It will take the train 2 hours to reach its destination.

Chapter 4: Mathematics Knowledge

The Math Knowledge (MK) section tests various concepts in numbers and operations, algebra, geometry, data analysis, statistics, and probability. In this test section, you will be provided with 25 questions to answer within a 24-minutes time limit, which gives you a little over a minute to solve each problem. This seems like less time than it actually is, so don't worry! Before you take the ASVAB, you want to make sure that you have a good understanding of the math areas which will be covered. You will need to sharpen your skills, but don't worry – we'll provide you with the knowledge that you'll need to know for the test.

Math Concepts Tested

You have a much better chance of getting a good Math Knowledge score if you know what to expect. The test covers math up to and including the first semester of Algebra II as well as fundamental geometry. You will not be given any formulas, such as those required for geometry calculations, so you need to make sure that you have studied them so they are fresh in your mind.

Here is a breakdown of areas covered:

Numbers and Operations
- Absolute values, inequalities, probabilities, exponents, and radicals.

Algebra and Functions
- Basic equation solving, simultaneous equations, binomials & polynomials, and inequalities.

Geometry and Measurement
- Angle relationships, area and perimeter of geometric shapes, and volume.

Math skills that you won't need:

- Working with bulky numbers or endless calculations.
- Working with imaginary numbers or the square roots of negative numbers.
- Trigonometry or calculus.

Note: You are not allowed to use a calculator for any section of the ASVAB.

The Most Common Mistakes

Here is a list of the four most commonly- made mistakes concerning mathematics, starting with the most common.
1. Answer is the wrong sign (positive / negative).
2. Order of Operations not following when solving.
3. Misplaced decimal.
4. Solution is not what the question asked for.

These are the basics that individuals tend to overlook when they only have a minute or less to do their calculations. This is why it is so important that you pay attention right from the start of the problem. You may be thinking, "But, those are just common sense." Exactly! Remember, even simple mistakes still result in an incorrect answer.

In the computer version of the ASVAB, there is no opportunity to go back and fix your mistakes. Once you make your answer choice and move on to the next question, there is no going back.

Strategies

- Review the Basics: First and foremost, practice your basic skills such as sign changes, order of operations, simplifying fractions, and equation manipulation. These are the skills you will use the most on almost every problem on the Math Knowledge and the Arithmetic tests sections. Remember when it comes right down to it, there are still only four math operations used to solve any math problem, which are adding, subtracting, multiplying and dividing; the only thing that changes is the order they are used to solve the problem.

- Although accuracy counts more than speed; don't waste time stuck on a question! Remember, you only have 24 minutes to answer 25 questions for this section test. This is why your knowledge of the basics is so important. If you have to stop and think about what 9 * 6 equals, or use your fingers to add 13 + 8, then you need to spend time on these fundamentals before going on to the concepts. There are minute tests at the end of this chapter. If you can complete those tests in the time specified, the time required for you to calculate the more complex problems during the test will decrease greatly.

- Make an educated guess: If necessary, eliminate at least one answer choice as most probably incorrect and guess which one is most likely correct from the remaining choices.

Math Formulas, Facts, and Terms that You Need to Know

The next few pages will cover the various math subjects (starting with the basics, but in no particular order) along with worked examples. Use this guide to determine the areas in which you need more review and work these areas first. You should take your time at first and let your brain recall the math necessary to solve the problems, using the examples given to remember these skills.

Order of Operations	**PEMDAS** – **P**arentheses/**E**xponents/**M**ultiply/**D**ivide/**A**dd/**S**ubtract

Perform the operations within parentheses first, then any exponents. Then do all multiplication and division. These are done from left to right as they appear in the problem; this is followed by addition and subtraction, also from left to right as they appear in the problem.

Examples:

Solve $(-(2)^2 - (4 + 7))$
$(-4 - 11) = -15$

Solve $((5)^2 \div 5 + 4 * 2)$
$25 \div 5 + 4 * 2$
$5 + 8 = 13$

Positive & Negative Number Rules

$(+) + (-) =$ subtract the two numbers, the sign of the larger number stays
$(-) + (-) =$ negative number
$(-) * (-) =$ positive number
$(-) \div (-) =$ positive number
$(-) \div (+) =$ negative number
$(-) * (+) =$ negative number

Absolute Value

The absolute value of a number is its distance from zero, not its value.
$|x| = a$
$x = -a$ and $x = a$

$|3| = 3$
and
$|-3| = 3$

For equations with absolute values you will have two answers.
Each must be solved separately and all solutions must be checked into the original equation.

Ex: Solve for x: $|2x - 3| = x + 1$

$$2x - 3 = -(x + 1) \qquad \text{and} \qquad 2x - 3 = x + 1$$
$$2x - 3 = -x - 1 \qquad\qquad\qquad\qquad x = 4$$
$$3x = 2$$
$$x = 2/3$$

Fractions

Adding and subtracting fractions requires a common denominator.

$$\frac{4}{5} + \frac{2}{5} = \frac{6}{5} = 1\frac{1}{5}$$

To find a common denominator:

$$\frac{2}{3} - \frac{1}{5} = \frac{2}{3}\left(\frac{5}{5}\right) - \frac{1}{5}\left(\frac{3}{3}\right) = \frac{10}{15} - \frac{3}{15} = \frac{7}{15}$$

To add mixed fractions, work the whole numbers, then the fractions:

Ex: $2\frac{1}{4} + 1\frac{3}{4} = 3\frac{4}{4} = 4$

To subtract mixed fractions, convert to single fractions by multiplying the whole number by the denominator and adding the numerator, then work as above:

Ex: $2\frac{1}{4} - 1\frac{3}{4} = \frac{9}{4} - \frac{7}{4} = \frac{2}{4} = \frac{1}{2}$

To multiply fractions, convert any mixed fractions into single fractions and multiply across; reduce to lowest terms if needed.

Ex: $2\frac{1}{4} * 1\frac{3}{4} = \frac{9}{4} * \frac{7}{4} = \frac{63}{16} = 3\frac{15}{16}$

To divide fractions, convert any mixed fractions into single fractions, flip the second fraction, then multiply across.

Ex: $2\frac{1}{4} \div 1\frac{3}{4} = \frac{9}{4} \div \frac{7}{4} = \frac{9}{4} * \frac{4}{7} = \frac{36}{28} = 1\frac{8}{28} = 1\frac{2}{7}$

TEST SECRET

Check the answer choices to see if you need to reduce the fraction to its lowest terms.

Arithmetic Sequence
Each term is equal to the previous term plus x.
Ex: 2, 5, 8, 11   2+3=5; 5+3=8 … etc. $x = 3$

Geometric Sequence
Each term is equal to the previous term multiplied by x
Ex: 2, 4, 8, 16 $x = 2$

Prime Factorization
Expand to prime number factors.
Ex: $104 = 2 * 2 * 2 * 13$

Greatest Common Factor (GCF)
Multiply common prime factors.
Ex: $28 = 2 * 2 * 7$
$80 = 2 * 2 * 2 * 5$

$GCF = 2 * 2 = 4$

Mean, Median, Mode

Mean is a math term for "average". Total all terms and divide by the number of terms number of terms.

Ex: Find the average of 24, 27, 18

$24 + 27 + 18 = 69$ $69 \div 3 = 23$

Median is the middle number of a given set after they have been put in numerical order. In the case of a set of even numbers, the middle two numbers are averaged.

Ex: What is the median of 24, 27, and 18?

18, 24, 27 the median is 24

Mode is the number that occurs most frequently within a given set.

Ex: What is the mode of 2,5,4,4,3,2,8,9,2,7,2,2

The mode would be 2 because it appears four times in the set.

Combining like terms

This is exactly how it sounds! When a variable (x, y, z, r – anything!) is present in an equation, you can combine those terms with like variables.

$9r + 2r = 11r$

$4x + 2y + 3 - 2x = 2x + 2y + 3$

Distributive property

When a variable is placed outside of a parenthetical set, it is *distributed* to all of the variables within that set.

$5(2y - 3x) = 10y - 15x$ (can also be written as $(2y - 3x)5$)

$2x(3y + 1) + 6x = 6xy + 2x + 6x = 6xy + 8x$

Exponent Rules

- $x^0 = 1$ Example: $5^0 = 1$
- $x^1 = x$ Example: $5^1 = 5$
- $x^a \cdot x^b = x^{a+b}$ Example: $5^2 * 5^3 = 5^5$
- $(xy)^a = x^a y^a$ Example: $(5 * 6)^2 = 5^2 * 6^2 = 25 * 36$
- $(x^a)^b = x^{ab}$ Example: $(5^2)^3 = 5^6$
- $(x/y)^a = x^a / y^a$ Example: $(10/5)^2 = 10^2 / 5^2 = 100/25$
- $x^a / y^b = x^{a-b}$ Example: $5^4 / 5^3 = 5^1 = 5$ (remember $x \neq 0$)
- $x^{1/a} = \sqrt[a]{x}$ Example: $25^{1/2} = \sqrt[2]{25} = 5$
- $x^{-a} = \dfrac{1}{x^a}$ Example: $5^{-2} = \dfrac{1}{5^2} = \dfrac{1}{25}$ (remember $x \neq 0$)

- $(-x)^a$ = positive number if "a" is even; negative number if "a" is odd

Ex: Simplify $\dfrac{(3^{-1}a^4 b^{-3})^{-2}}{(6a^2 ab^{-1}c^{-2})^2}$

$$\frac{(3^{-1}a^4 b^{-3})^{-2}}{(6a^2 ab^{-1}c^{-2})} = \frac{3^2 a^{-8} b^6}{6^2 a^6 b^{-2} c^{-4}}$$

$$= \frac{9a^{-8} b^6}{36 a^6 b^{-2} c^{-4}} = \frac{b^6 b^2 c^4}{4a^6 a^8} = \frac{b^8 c^4}{4a^{14}}$$

Answer $= \dfrac{b^8 c^4}{4a^{14}}$

Ex: Simplify $[(3x^4 y^7 z^{12})^5 (-5x^9 y^3 z^4)^2]^0$

Stop! Put down your thinking cap – there's no need to figure out all of that within the brackets. See how the overall exponent is 0?

The answer is 1. Remember $x^0 = 1$

Roots

Root of a Product: $\sqrt[n]{a \cdot b} = \sqrt[n]{a} \cdot \sqrt[n]{b}$

Root of a Quotient: $\sqrt[n]{\dfrac{a}{b}} = \dfrac{\sqrt[n]{a}}{\sqrt[n]{b}}$

Fractional Exponent: $\sqrt[n]{a^m} = a^{m/n}$

Ex: Simplify $\dfrac{2(6-3\sqrt{5})}{(6+3\sqrt{5})(6-3\sqrt{5})}$

$$= \dfrac{12-6\sqrt{5}}{6^2 - (3\sqrt{5})^2}$$

$$= \dfrac{12-6\sqrt{5}}{6^2 - (3\sqrt{5})^2} = \dfrac{12-6\sqrt{5}}{6^2 - (3\times 3\times \sqrt{5}\times \sqrt{5})}$$

$$= \dfrac{12-6\sqrt{5}}{6^2 - (9\times 5)} = \dfrac{12-6\sqrt{5}}{36-45} = \dfrac{12-6\sqrt{5}}{-9} = -\dfrac{(12-6\sqrt{5})}{9}$$

$$= -\dfrac{3(4-2\sqrt{5})}{9} = -\dfrac{(4-2\sqrt{5})}{3} = \dfrac{-4+2\sqrt{5}}{3}$$

Answer $= \dfrac{-4+2\sqrt{5}}{3}$

Algebraic Equations

When simplifying or solving algebraic equations, you need to be able to utilize all math rules: exponents, roots, negatives, order of operations, etc.

1. Add & Subtract only the coefficients of like terms:

Ex: $5xy +7y + 2yz + 11xy - 5yz = 16xy + 7y - 3yz$

2. Multiplication: First the coefficients then the variables:

Ex:

monomial * monomial

$(3x^4y^2z)(2y^4z^5) = 6x^4y^6z^6$

(A variable with no exponent has an implied exponent of 1)

Ex:

monomial * polynomial

$(2y^2)(y^3+2xy^2z + 4z) = 2y^5 + 4xy^4z + 8y^2z$

Ex:

binomial * binomial

$(5x + 2)(3x + 3)$

(Remember FOIL – First, Outer, Inner, Last)

First $5x * 3x = 15x^2$

Outer $5x * 3 = 15x$

Inner $2 * 3x = 6x$

Last $2 * 3 = 6$

Combine like terms: $15x^2 + 21x + 6$

Ex:

binomial * polynomial

$(x + 3)(2x^2 – 5x – 2)$

First term $x(2x^2 – 5x – 2) = 2x^3 – 5x^2 – 2x$

Second term $3(2x^2 – 5x – 2) = 6x^2 – 15x – 6$

Added Together $2x^3 + x^2 – 17x – 6$

Inequalities

Inequalities are solved like linear and algebraic equations, except the sign must be reversed when dividing by a negative number.

Ex:
Solve: $-7x + 2 < 6 – 5x$
Step 1: Combine like terms. $-2x < 4$
Step 2: Solve for x. Reverse sign. $x > -2$

Solving compound inequalities will give you two answers.

Ex:
Solve: $-4 \le 2x – 2 \le 6$
Step 1: Add 2 to each term to isolate x $-2 \le 2x \le 8$
Step 2: Divide by 2. $-1 \le x \le 4$

Solution set is [-1, 4]

Literal Equations   Equations with more than one variable. Solve in terms of one variable first.

Ex:
Solve for y: $4x + 3y = 3x + 2y$

Step 1: Combine like terms. $3y - 2y = 4x - 2x$
Step 2: Solve for y. $y = 2x$

Linear Systems

There are two different methods can be used to solve multiple equation linear systems on the ASVAB.

Substitution method: This solves for one variable in one equation and substitutes it into the other equation.

Ex:
Solve: $3y - 4 + x = 0$ and $5x + 6y = 11$

Step 1: Solve for one variable:

$$3y - 4 = 0$$
$$3y + x = 4$$
$$x = 4 - 3y$$

Step 2: Substitute into second equation and solve:

$$5(4 - 3y) + 6y = 11$$
$$20 - 15y + 6y = 11$$
$$20 - 9y = 11$$
$$-9y = -9$$
$$y = 1$$

Step 3: Substitute into first equation:

$$3(1) - 4 + x = 0$$
$$-1 + x = 0$$
$$x = 1$$

Solution: $x = 1, y = 1$

Addition method: Manipulate one of the equations so that when it is added to the other, one variable is eliminated.

Ex:
Solve: $2x + 4y = 8$ and $4x + 2y = 10$

Step 1:
Manipulate one equation to eliminate a variable when added together:

$$-2(2x + 4y = 8)$$
$$-4x - 8y = -16$$
$$(-4x - 8y = -16) + (4x + 2y = 10)$$
$$-6y = -6$$
$$y = 1$$

Step 2: Plug into an equation to solve for the other variable:

$$2x + 4(1) = 8$$
$$2x + 4 = 8$$
$$2x = 4$$
$$x = 2$$

Solution: $x = 2$, $y = 1$

Slope (m)

The formula used to calculate the slope (m) of a straight line connecting two points is: $m = (y_2 - y_1) / (x_2 - x_1)$ = change in y /change in x.

Ex:
Calculate slope of the line in the diagram:

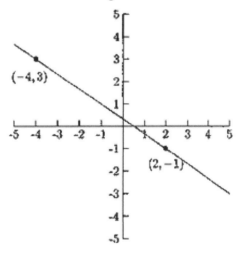

$m = (3 - (-1))/(-4 - 2) = 4/-6 = -2/3$

TEST SECRET

Remember, when calculating slope, it isn't important which point you designate (x1,y1) as long as you are consistent throughout your problem.

Midpoint

To determine the midpoint between two points, simply add the two x coordinates together and divide by 2 (midpoint x) and add the y coordinates together and divide by 2 (midpoint y).

$$\left(\frac{x_1 + x_2}{2}, \frac{y_1 + y}{2}\right)$$

Quadratics

Factoring: Converting $ax^2 + bx + c$ to factored form. Find two numbers that are factors of c and whose sum is b.

Ex:
Factor: $2x^2 + 12x + 18 = 0$
Step 1: If possible, factor out a common monomial:

$$2(x^2 - 6x + 9)$$

Step 2: Find two numbers that are factors of 9 and which equal -6 when added:

$$2(x\ \ )(x\ \ )$$
$$-3\ \ , -3$$

Step 3: Fill in the binomials. Be sure to check your answer signs.
$$2(x - 3)(x - 3)$$

Step 4: To solve, set each to equal 0.
$$x - 3 = 0$$
$$\text{so}\ \ x = 3$$

Difference of squares.
$$a^2 - b^2 = (a + b)(a - b)$$
$$a^2 + 2ab + b^2 = (a + b)(a + b)$$
$$a^2 - 2ab + b^2 = (a - b)(a - b)$$

TEST SECRET

If c is positive and b is positive, then the factors will both be positive. If c is positive and b is negative, then the factors will both be negative. If c is negative, the factors will have opposite signs.

(The number of possibilities of an event happening) * (the number of possibilities of another event happening) = the total number of possibilities.

Fundamental Counting Principle	Ex: If you take a multiple choice test with 5 questions, with 4 answer choices for each question, how many test result possibilities are there? Solution: Question 1 has 4 choices; question 2 has 4 choices; etc. 4 * 4 * 4 * 4 * 4 (one for each question) = 1024 possible test results.
Permutations	The number of ways a set number of items can be arranged. Recognized by the use of a factorial (n!), with n being the number of items. If n = 3, then 3! = 3 * 2 * 1 = 6. If you need to arrange n number of things but *x* number are alike, then n! is divided by *x*! Ex: How many different ways can the letters in the word **balance** be arranged? Solution: There are 7 letters so *n! = 7!* and 2 letters are the same so *x! = 2!* Set up the equation: $$\frac{7*6*5*4*3*2*1}{2*1} = 2540 \text{ ways}$$
Combinations	To calculate total number of possible combinations use the formula: n!/r! (n-r)! n = # of objects r = # of objects selected at a time Ex: If seven people are selected in groups of three, how many different combinations are possible? Solution: $$\frac{7*6*5*4*3*2*1}{(3*2*1)(7-3)} = 210 \text{ possible combinations}$$
Probabilities	A probability is found by dividing the number of desired outcomes by the number of possible outcomes. (The piece divided by the whole.) Ex: What is the probability of picking a blue marble if 3 of the 15 marbles are blue? Answer: 3/15 = 1/5. The probability is 1 in 5 that a blue marble is picked.

Geometry

The MK section only requires knowledge of basic geometry; most of which you likely learned in the eighth grade. You will need to be familiar with basic angle and shape terminology as well as basic formulas.

Acute angle:
Measures less than 90°

Acute triangle:
Each angle measures less than 90°

Right angle:
Measures exactly 90^0

Right triangle:
One angle measures exactly 90^0

Obtuse angle:
Measures greater than 90°

Obtuse triangle:
One angle measures greater than 90°

Radius and Circumference of a Circle:

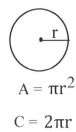

$$A = \pi r^2$$

$$C = 2\pi r$$

Area of a rectangle:

$$A = lw$$

Area of a Triangle:

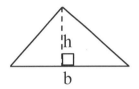

$$A = \frac{1}{2} bh$$

Volume of a Cube:

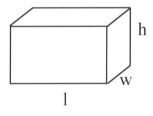

$$V = lwh$$

Volume of a Cylinder:

$$V = \pi r^2 h$$

The Pythagorean Theorem:

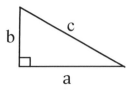

$$c^2 = a^2 + b^2$$

Special Right Triangles:

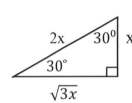 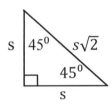

The number of degrees of an arc in a circle is 360°.

The measure of degrees of a straight angle is 180°.

The sum of degrees of the angles in a triangle is 180°.

Make sure you are familiar with using these equations, including manipulating them. For example:

If A = 1/2bh, then h = (2A)/b

Practice Drill: Mathematics Knowledge

ORDER OF OPERATIONS

1. $3 * (2 * 4^3) \div 4 = $ _____

2. $(4^3 + 2 - 1) = $ _____

3. $(5 * 3) * 1 + 5 = $ _____

4. $(7^2 - 2^3 - 6) = $ _____

5. $(5^3 + 7) * 2 = $ _____

ALGEBRA

6. If Lynn can type a page in *p* minutes, how many pages can she do in 5 minutes?
  a) $5/p$.
  b) $p - 5$.
  c) $p + 5$.
  d) $p/5$.
  e) $1 - p + 5$.

7. If Sally can paint a house in 4 hours, and John can paint the same house in 6 hours, then how long will it take for both of them to paint the house together?
  a) 2 hours and 24 minutes.
  b) 3 hours and 12 minutes.
  c) 3 hours and 44 minutes.
  d) 4 hours and 10 minutes.
  e) 4 hours and 33 minutes.

8. The sales price of a car is $12,590, which is 20% off the original price. What is the original price?
  a) $14,310.40.
  b) $14,990.90.
  c) $15,290.70.
  d) $15,737.50.
  e) $16,935.80.

9. Solve the following equation for *a*: $2a \div 3 = 8 + 4a$.
  a) -2.4.
  b) 2.4.
  c) 1.3.
  d) -1.3.
  e) 0.

10. If $y = 3$, then what is $y^3(y^3 - y)$?

    a) 300.

    b) 459.

    c) 648.

    d) 999.

    e) 1099.

ALGEBRA 2

11. The average of three numbers is v. If one of the numbers is z and another is y, then what is the remaining number?

    a) $ZY - V$.

    b) $Z/V - 3 - Y$.

    c) $Z/3 - V - Y$.

    d) $3V - Z - Y$.

    e) $V - Z - Y$.

12. Mary is reviewing her algebra quiz. She has determined that one of her solutions is incorrect. Which one is it?

    a) $2x + 5(x - 1) = 9$; $x = 2$.

    b) $p - 3(p - 5) = 10$; $p = 2.5$.

    c) $4y + 3y = 28$; $y = 4$.

    d) $5w + 6w - 3w = 64$; $w = 8$.

    e) $t - 2t - 3t = 32$; $t = 8$.

13. What simple interest rate will Susan need to secure in order to make \$2,500 in interest on a \$10,000 principal over 5 years?

    a) 4%.

    b) 5%.

    c) 6%.

    d) 7%.

    e) 8%.

14. Which of the following is not a rational number?

    a) -4.

    b) $1/5$.

    c) $0.8333333...$

    d) 0.45.

    e) $\sqrt{2}$.

AVERAGES and ROUNDING

15. Round 907.457 to the nearest tens place.
    a) 908.0.
    b) 910.
    c) 907.5.
    d) 900.
    e) 907.46.

16. What is 1230.932567 rounded to the nearest hundredths place?
    a) 1200.
    b) 1230.9326.
    c) 1230.93.
    d) 1230.
    e) 1230.933.

17. Subtract the following numbers and round to the nearest tenths place:
134.679
− 45.548
− 67.8807

    a) 21.3.
    b) 21.25.
    c) -58.97.
    d) -59.0.
    e) 1.

18. What is the absolute value of –9?
    a) –9.
    b) 9.
    c) 0.
    d) –1.
    e) 1.

19. What is the median of the following list of numbers: 4, 5, 7, 9, 10, and 12?
    a) 6.
    b) 7.5.
    c) 7.8.
    d) 8.
    e) 9.

20. What is the mathematical average of the number of weeks in a year, seasons in a year, and the number of days in January?
    a) 36.
    b) 33.
    c) 32.
    d) 31.
    e) 29.

BASIC OPERATIONS

21. Add 0.98 + 45.102 + 32.3333 + 31 + 0.00009.
- a) 368.573.
- b) 210.536299.
- c) 109.41539.
- d) 99.9975.
- e) 80.8769543.

22. Find 0.12 ÷ 1.
- a) 12.
- b) 1.2.
- c) .12.
- d) .012.
- e) .0012.

23. (9 ÷ 3) * (8 ÷ 4) equals:
- a) 1.
- b) 6.
- c) 72.
- d) 576.
- e) 752.

24. 6 * 0 * 5 equals:
- a) 30.
- b) 11.
- c) 25.
- d) 0.
- e) 27.

25. 7.95 ÷ 1.5 equals:
- a) 2.4.
- b) 5.3.
- c) 6.2.
- d) 7.3.
- e) 7.5.

ESTIMATION SEQUENCE

26. Describe the following sequence in mathematical terms: 144, 72, 36, 18, and 9.
- a) Descending arithmetic sequence.
- b) Ascending arithmetic sequence.
- c) Descending geometric sequence.
- d) Ascending geometric sequence.
- e) Miscellaneous sequence.

27. Which of the following is not a whole number followed by its square?

    a) 1, 1.
    b) 6, 36.
    c) 8, 64.
    d) 10, 100.
    e) 11, 144.

28. There are 12 more apples than oranges in a basket of 36 apples and oranges. How many apples are in the basket?

    a) 12.
    b) 15.
    c) 24.
    d) 28.
    e) 36.

29. Which of the following correctly identifies 4 consecutive odd integers, where the sum of the middle two integers is equal to 24?

    a) 5, 7, 9, 11.
    b) 7, 9, 11, 13.
    c) 9, 11, 13, 15.
    d) 11, 13, 15, 17.
    e) 13, 15, 17, 19.

30. What is the next number in the sequence? 6, 12, 24, 48, ___.

    a) 72.
    b) 96.
    c) 108.
    d) 112.
    e) 124.

MEASUREMENT PRACTICE

31. If a rectangular house has a perimeter of 44 yards, and a length of 36 feet, what is the house's width?

    a) 30 feet.
    b) 18 yards.
    c) 28 feet.
    d) 32 feet.
    e) 36 yards.

32. What is the volume of a cylinder with a diameter of 1 foot and a height of 14 inches?

    a) 2104.91cubic inches.
    b) 1584 cubic inches.
    c) 528 cubic inches.
    d) 904.32 cubic inches.
    e) 264 cubic inches.

33. What is the volume of a cube whose width is 5 inches?
   a) 15 cubic inches.
   b) 25 cubic inches.
   c) 64 cubic inches.
   d) 100 cubic inches.
   e) 125 cubic inches.

34. A can's diameter is 3 inches, and its height is 8 inches. What is the volume of the can?
   a) 50.30 cubic inches.
   b) 56.57 cubic inches.
   c) 75.68 cubic inches.
   d) 113.04 cubic inches.
   e) 226.08 cubic inches.

35. If the area of a square flowerbed is 16 square feet, then how many feet is the flowerbed's perimeter?
   a) 4.
   b) 12.
   c) 16.
   d) 20.
   e) 24.

PERCENT and RATIO

36. If a discount of 25% off the retail price of a desk saves Mark $45, what was desk's original price?
   a) $135.
   b) $160.
   c) $180.
   d) $210.
   e) $215.

37. A customer pays $1,100 in state taxes on a newly-purchased car. What is the value of the car if state taxes are 8.9% of the value?
   a) $9.765.45.
   b) $10,876.90.
   c) $12,359.55.
   d) $14,345.48.
   e) $15,745.45.

38. How many years does Steven need to invest his $3,000 at 7% to earn $210 in simple interest?
   a) 1 year.
   b) 2 years.
   c) 3 years.
   d) 4 years.
   e) 5 years.

39. 35% of what number is 70?
   a) 100.
   b) 110.
   c) 150.
   d) 175.
   e) 200.

40. What number is 5% of 2000?
   a) 50.
   b) 100.
   c) 150.
   d) 200.
   e) 250.

COMBINED MATHEMATIC CONCEPTS PRACTICE

41. How long will Lucy have to wait before for her $2,500 invested at 6% earns $600 in simple interest?
   a) 2 years.
   b) 3 years.
   c) 4 years.
   d) 5 years.
   e) 6 years.

42. If $r = 5z$ and $15z = 3y$, then r equals:
   a) y.
   b) $2y$.
   c) $5y$.
   d) $10y$.
   e) $15y$.

43. What is 35% of a number if 12 is 15% of that number?
   a) 5.
   b) 12.
   c) 28.
   d) 33.
   e) 62.

44. A computer is on sale for $1,600, which is a 20% discount off the regular price. The regular price is?
   a) $1800.
   b) $1900.
   c) $2000.
   d) $2100.
   e) $2200.

45. **A car dealer sells an SUV for $39,000, which represents a 25% profit over the cost. What was the cost of the SUV to the dealer?**
    a) $29,250.
    b) $31,200.
    c) $32,500.
    d) $33,800.
    e) $33,999.

46. **Employees of a discount appliance store receive an additional 20% off of the lowest price on an item. If an employee purchases a dishwasher during a 15% off sale, how much will he pay if the dishwasher originally cost $450?**
    a) $280.90.
    b) $287.
    c) $292.50.
    d) $306.
    e) $333.89.

47. **The city council has decided to add a 0.3% tax on motel and hotel rooms. If a traveler spends the night in a motel room that costs $55 before taxes, how much will the city receive in taxes from him?**
    a) 10 cents.
    b) 11 cents.
    c) 15 cents.
    d) 17 cents.
    e) 21 cents.

48. **Grace has 16 jellybeans in her pocket. She has 8 red ones, 4 green ones, and 4 blue ones. What is the minimum number of jellybeans she must take out of her pocket to ensure that she has one of each color?**
    a) 4.
    b) 8.
    c) 12.
    d) 13.
    e) 16.

49. **You need to purchase a textbook for nursing school. The book costs $80.00, and the sales tax is 8.25%. You have $100. How much change will you receive back?**
    a) $5.20.
    b) $7.35.
    c) $13.40.
    d) $19.95.
    e) $21.25.

50. Your supervisor instructs you to purchase 240 pens and 6 staplers for the nurse's station. Pens are purchased in sets of 6 for $2.35 per pack. Staplers are sold in sets of 2 for $12.95. How much will purchasing these products cost?
    a) $132.85.
    b) $145.75.
    c) $162.90.
    d) $225.25.
    e) $226.75.

51. Two cyclists start biking from a trailhead at different speeds and times. The second cyclist travels at 10 miles per hour and starts 3 hours after the first cyclist, who is traveling at 6 miles per hour. Once the second cyclist starts biking, how much time will pass before he catches up with the first cyclist?
    a) 2 hours.
    b) 4 ½ hours.
    c) 5 ¾ hours.
    d) 6 hours.
    e) 7 ½ hours.

52. Jim can fill a pool with water by the bucket-full in 30 minutes. Sue can do the same job in 45 minutes. Tony can do the same job in 1 ½ hours. How quickly can all three fill the pool together?
    a) 12 minutes.
    b) 15 minutes.
    c) 21 minutes.
    d) 23 minutes.
    e) 28 minutes.

53. A study reported that, in a random sampling of 100 women over the age of 35, 8 of the women had been married 2 or more times. Based on the study results, how many women over the age of 35 in a group of 5,000 would likely have been married 2 or more times?
    a) 55.
    b) 150.
    c) 200.
    d) 400.
    e) 600.

54. John is traveling to a meeting that is 28 miles away. He needs to be there in 30 minutes. How fast does he need to go in order to make it to the meeting on time?
    a) 25 mph.
    b) 37 mph.
    c) 41 mph.
    d) 49 mph.
    e) 56 mph.

55. If Steven can mix 20 drinks in 5 minutes, Sue can mix 20 drinks in 10 minutes, and Jack can mix 20 drinks in 15 minutes, then how much time will it take all 3 of them working together to mix the 20 drinks?
    a) 2 minutes and 44 seconds.
    b) 2 minutes and 58 seconds.
    c) 3 minutes and 10 seconds.
    d) 3 minutes and 26 seconds.
    e) 4 minutes and 15 seconds.

56. Jim's belt broke, and his pants are falling down. He has 5 pieces of string. He needs to choose the piece that will be able to go around his 36-inch waist. The piece must be at least 4 inches longer than his waist so that he can tie a knot in it, but it cannot be more that 6 inches longer so that the ends will not show from under his shirt. Which of the following pieces of string will work the best?
    a) 3 feet.
    b) 3 ¾ feet.
    c) 3 5/8 feet.
    d) 3 ¼ feet.
    e) 2 ½ feet.

57. In the final week of January, a car dealership sold 12 cars. A new sales promotion came out the first week of February, and the dealership sold 19 cars that week. What was the percent increase in sales from the last week of January compared to the first week of February?
    a) 58%.
    b) 119%.
    c) 158%.
    d) 175%.
    e) 200%.

58. If two planes leave the same airport at 1:00 PM, how many miles apart will they be at 3:00 PM if one travels directly north at 150 mph and the other travels directly west at 200 mph?
    a) 50 miles.
    b) 100 miles.
    c) 500 miles.
    d) 700 miles.
    e) 1,000 miles.

59. During a 5-day festival, the number of visitors tripled each day. If the festival opened on a Thursday with 345 visitors, what was the attendance on that Sunday?
    a) 345.
    b) 1,035.
    c) 1,725.
    d) 3,105.
    e) 9,315.

60. What will it cost to carpet a room with indoor/outdoor carpet if the room is 10 feet wide and 12 feet long? The carpet costs $12.51 per square yard.
    a) $166.80.
    b) $175.90.
    c) $184.30.
    d) $189.90.
    e) $192.20.

61. Sally has three pieces of material. The first piece is 1 yard, 2 feet, and 6 inches long; the second piece is 2 yard, 1 foot, and 5 inches long; and the third piece is 4 yards, 2 feet, and 8 inches long. How much material does Sally have?
    a) 7 yards, 1 foot, and 8 inches.
    b) 8 yards, 4 feet, and 4 inches.
    c) 8 yards and 11 inches.
    d) 9 yards and 7 inches.
    e) 10 yards.

62. A vitamin's expiration date has passed. It was supposed to contain 500 mg of Calcium, but it has lost 325 mg of Calcium. How many mg of Calcium are left?
    a) 135 mg.
    b) 175 mg.
    c) 185 mg.
    d) 200 mg.
    e) 220 mg.

63. You have orders to give a patient 20 mg of a certain medication. The medication is stored as 4 mg per 5-mL dose. How many milliliters will need to be given?
    a) 15 mL.
    b) 20 mL.
    c) 25 mL.
    d) 30 mL.
    e) 35 mL.

64. You need a 1680 ft^3 aquarium, exactly, for your fish. The pet store has four choices of aquariums. The length, width, and height are listed on the box, but not the volume. Which of the following aquariums would fit your needs?
    a) 12 ft by 12 ft by 12 ft.
    b) 13 ft by 15 ft by 16 ft.
    c) 14 ft by 20 ft by 6 ft.
    d) 15 ft by 16 ft by 12 ft.
    e) 15 ft by 12 ft by 12 ft.

65. Sabrina's boss states that she will increase Sabrina's salary from $12,000 to $14,000 per year if Sabrina enrolls in business courses at a local community college. What percent increase in salary will result from Sabrina taking the business courses?
    a) 15%.
    b) 16.7%.
    c) 17.2%.
    d) 85%.
    e) 117%.

66. Jim works for $15.50 per hour at a health care facility. He is supposed to get a $0.75 per hour raise after one year of service. What will be his percent increase in hourly pay?
    a) 2.7%.
    b) 3.3%.
    c) 133%.
    d) 4.8%.
    e) 105%.

67. Edmond has to sell his BMW. He bought the car for $49,000, but sold it at 20% less. At what price did Edmond sell the car?
    a) $24,200.
    b) $28,900.
    c) $35,600.
    d) $37,300.
    e) $39,200.

68. At a company fish fry, half of those in attendance are employees. Employees' spouses make up a third of the attendance. What is the percentage of the people in attendance who are neither employees nor employees' spouses?
    a) 10.5%.
    b) 16.7%.
    c) 25%.
    d) 32.3%.
    e) 38%.

69. If Sam can do a job in 4 days that Lisa can do in 6 days and Tom can do in 2 days, how long would the job take if Sam, Lisa, and Tom worked together to complete it?
    a) 0.8 days.
    b) 1.09 days.
    c) 1.23 days.
    d) 1.65 days.
    e) 1.97 days.

70. Sarah needs to make a cake and some cookies. The cake requires 3/8 cup of sugar, and the cookies require 3/5 cup of sugar. Sarah has 15/16 cups of sugar. Does she have enough sugar, or how much more does she need?

    a) She has enough sugar.
    b) She needs 1/8 of a cup of sugar.
    c) She needs 3/80 of a cup of sugar.
    d) She needs 4/19 of a cup of sugar.
    e) She needs 1/9 of a cup of sugar.

GEOMETRY

71. What is the area outside the circle, but within the square whose two corners are A and B?

A(3,5)   B (8,17)

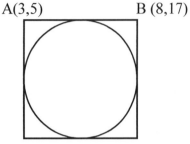

    a) $169(1-\pi)$
    b) 169π
    c) $169\pi/4$
    d) $169(1-\pi/4)$
    e) 169

72. What is the area, in square feet, of the triangle whose sides have lengths equal to 3, 4, and 5 feet?

    a) 6 square feet
    b) 7 square feet
    c) 4 square feet
    d) 5 square feet
    e) 8 square feet

73. In the following figure, where AE bisects line BC, and angles AEC and AEB are both right angles, what is the length of AB?

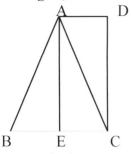

BC = 6 cm
AD = 3 cm
CD = 4 cm

  a) 1 cm
  b) 2 cm
  c) 3 cm
  d) 4 cm
  e) 5 cm

74. In the following triangle, if AB = 6 and BC = 8, what should the length of CA be to make triangle ABC a right triangle?

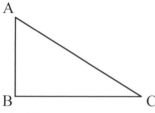

  a) 10
  b) 9
  c) 8
  d) 4
  e) 7

75. In the following circle there is a square with an area of 36 cm². What is the area outside the square, but within the circle?

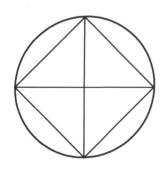

  a) 18π cm^2
  b) $18 \pi - 30$ cm^2
  c) $18 \pi - 36$ cm^2
  d) 18 cm^2
  e) -18 cm^2

1. **Answer: 96**
   Explanation: We need to remember the order of operations (PEMDAS) to solve this question. First of all, we solve the parenthesis, and then the exponents. In this particular question, 4^3 is within the parenthesis so we solve it first. $4^3 = 64$. Now, multiplying it with 2 to solve the parenthesis, it becomes $64*2 = 128$. So, the expression becomes $3*128÷4$. Following PEMDAS, we multiply 128 by 3, and then divide the answer by 4. This gives us $384÷4 = 96$

2. **Answer: 65**
   Explanation: We need to remember the order of operations (PEMDAS) to solve this question. First of all, we solve the parenthesis, and then the exponents. In this particular question, 4^3 is within the parenthesis so we solve it first. $4^3 = 64$. Now, the expression becomes (64+2-1). So, we add 2 in 64 first, and then subtract 1 from the answer. This gives us 66-1 = 5.

3. **Answer: 20**
   Explanation: This question also involves the order of operations (PEMDAS). To solve this question, we solve the parenthesis first, and then multiply the answer by 1. After that, we add 5 to get our final answer. (5*3) = 15, so the expression becomes 15*1+5 = 15 + 5 = 20

4. **Answer: 35**
   Explanation: We need to remember the order of operations (PEMDAS) to solve this question. First of all, we solve the parenthesis, and then the exponents. However, in order to solve the parenthesis, we need to know the values of 7^2 and 2^3. Therefore, we find these exponents first and then proceed with PEMDAS. Since $7^2 = 49$ and $2^3 = 8$, the expression becomes (49-8-6) i.e. we simply subtract 6 and 8 from 49 to get our final answer which is equal to 35.

5. **Answer: 264**
   Explanation: First of all, we find the value of 5^3 to solve the parenthesis (remember the order of operations PEMDAS). As we know that $5^3 = 5*5*5 = 125$, the expression becomes (125+7)*2. We solve the parenthesis first because it is given more preference in PEMDAS, it becomes132*2. Multiplying these two numbers, we get our final answer which is 264.

6. **Answer: Option(a)**
   Explanation: From the given information in the question, Lynn writes one page in 'p' minutes. Now, we are asked about the number of pages Lynn can write in 5 minutes. The simplest way to solve this question is by writing it in ratio form I.e.
   1 page ➜ 'p' minutes
   X pages ➜ 5 minutes
   Cross multiplying the above equations, we get 5*1 =x*p
   Therefore, x = 5/p (Which means that he can type 5/p pages in 5 minutes)

7. **Answer: Option (a)**
   Explanation: Sally can paint a house in 4 hours means that in one hour, Sally paints ¼ of the house. Similarly, John can paint a house in 6 hours, which means that he paints $\frac{1}{6}$ of the house in 1 hour. If both Sally and John work together for one hour, they can paint (1/4 + 1/6) = 5/12 of the house. In order to paint the house completely, they would need 12/5 hours. Please note that 12/5 = 2.4 hours. If we multiply 2.4 with 60, we can find out the exact number of minutes they are taking. 2.4 * 60 = 144 minutes. From the given answer options, only answer (a) correspond to 144 minutes (i.e. 2 hours and 24 minutes).

8. Answer: Option (d)

Explanation: The sales price of the car is 20% off the original price (20% discount) which means that the given price of $12590 is 80% of the original price. Let's say that 'x' is the original price of the car, then

(80/100)*x = 12590 (i.e. 80% of 'x' equals $12590)
Solving the above equation, x = 12590*(100/80) ➜ $15,737 Option (d)

9. Answer: Option (a)

Explanation: We re-write this equation as $\frac{2a}{3}$ = 8+4a. Now, we multiply by 3 on both sides. The equation becomes 2a = 24 + 12a ➜ -24 = 10a ➜ **a= -2.4** Option (a)

10. Answer: Option (c)

Explanation: It's a relatively simple question. The value of 'y' is given as 3. We know that 3^3 = 27. So, the expression becomes 27 * (27-3) = 27*24 ➜ **648** Option (c)

11. Answer: Option (d)

Explanation: Let's suppose that the unknown number is 'w'. So, the average of three numbers becomes,

$\frac{W+Z+Y}{3}$ = V

Multiplying by '3' on both sides, we get
w+z+y = 3v
W= 3v-z-y
So, the unknown number equals 3V- Z -Y

12. Answer: Option (e)

Explanation: In these types of questions, we have to check each answer option to find out the desired answer. In this particular question, we are looking for the option which gives INCORRECT answer. (It's very important that you read the statement of the question correctly)

Option(a) ➜ 2(2) + 5(2-1) = 4+ 5 =9 Which gives the correct answer.
Option (b)➜ 2.5- 3(2.5 -5) = 10 which gives the correct answer.
Option (c)➜ 4(4)+ 3(4) = 28 which gives the correct answer
Option (d) ➜ 5(8) + 6(8) -3(8) = 64 which gives the correct answer
Option (e) ➜ 8 – 2(8) – 3(8) = -32 ≠ 32. Option (e) gives us incorrect answer, therefore, we choose this option.

13. Answer: Option (b)

Explanation: The principal amount is given as $10,000 and the total interest generated on this amount in 5 years is $2500. If we suppose that 'x' is the percentage of interest per year, then the equation becomes,
5 * (x/100) * 10000 = 2500
Solving for 'x', we get x = 5%.

14. Answer: Option (e)

Explanation: A rational number is the one which can be written in form of a simple fraction. If we observe closely, only option (e) gives us a number which cannot be written in form of a fraction.

15. Answer: Option (b)

Explanation: We are asked to round off 907.457 to the nearest tens place. As the tens place in 907.457 is '7' which is greater than 5, we make is 910.

16. Answer: Option (c)

Explanation: We are asked to round off this given number to the nearest hundredth place. Considering the numbers on the right of the decimal, our answer comes out to be 1230.93

17. Answer: Option (a)

Explanation: When we subtract 45.548 and 67.8807 from 134.679, we get 21.2503. Now, applying the rounding off rules, 21.3 (Note that we were asked to round off upto the nearest tenth place only)

18. Answer: Option (b)

Explanation: We know that the absolute value of any negative number gives the positive of that same number i.e. Absolute value of -9 is +9.

19. Answer: Option (d)

Explanation: In order to find the median of any given list, first of all, we need to check if the numbers are arranged in an ascending order or not. In this case, these given numbers are already arranged in order. Secondly, we need to check if the total number of entries in the list is even or odd. Since the total number of entries in this list is 6, and 6 is an even number, the median of this list equals the average of two entries which are at the middle of this list. i.e. Median $=\frac{7+9}{2} = 8$.

20. Answer: Option (e)

Explanation: We know that the total number of weeks in a year is 52, the total number of seasons in a year is 4, and the total number of days in month of January is 31. Taking average of these 3 numbers, we get
$\frac{52+4+31}{3} = 29$

21. Answer: Option (c)

Explanation: There are two ways to solve this question. Either you can add all the given numbers and find the exact answer. This method is time consuming and is less efficient.
The second method to solve this question is by adding only the numbers on the left of the decimal and then comparing your answer with the answer choices that you are given. We add 45, 32 and 31 to get 45+32+31 = 108. Now, we can easily interpret that our answer must be very close to 108 when we add the decimal points as well for each given number. In the answer choices, Only option (c) gives us a number which is closest to 108. (Note that this method of approximation saves time but it is not very accurate if all the answer choices are very close to each other.)

22. Answer: Option (c)

Explanation: Any number divided by '1' gives the same number as a result. Therefore, 0.12/1 = 0.12

23. Answer: Option (b)

Explanation: This is a very simple question. All you need to know is PEMDAS rule. First of all, we solve what is within the parenthesis, and then we multiply the answers of each parenthesis.
9 divided by 3 equals 3.
8 divided by 4 equals 2.
We multiply 3 and 2 to get our final answer: 3*2 = 6

24. Answer: Option (d)

Explanation: Anything multiplied by zero gives zero as answer. We are multiplying 0 by 5 and 6, so the answer is still 0.

25. Answer: Option (b)

Explanation: It is a simple division question. When we divide 7.95 by 1.5, we get 5.3 as answer. In order to re-confirm your answer, you can cross check by multiplying 5.3 by 1.5, and it would give 7.95.

26. Answer: Option (c)

Explanation: From the given sequence of numbers, we note that the numbers start from the highest and gradually decrease (144 > 72 > 36 18 > 9). Because of this decreasing order, we are sure that these numbers are in descending order. Also, we note that every next number in this sequence is obtained by dividing the previous number by 2. Therefore, it is Descending Geometric Sequence. (Some students might confuse it with geometric sequence with arithmetic sequence but please note that, for a sequence to be arithmetic, the difference between any two consecutive numbers in that sequence must be the same.)

27. Answer: Option (e)

Explanation: We know that $11^2 = 121$ ➔ $121 \neq 144$.

Option (e) is 11, 144. Since we are to choose the option in which a whole number is not followed by its square, and we know that $11^2 = 121$ instead of 144, we select option(e).

28. Answer: Option (c)

Explanation: Let's suppose that there are 'x' oranges in the basket. From the given statement of the question, the number of apples is 12 more than the number of oranges i.e. x+12. Also, its given that the total number of apples and oranges is 36. Writing this information in form of an equation, it becomes:

x+ x+12 = 36

2x= 36-12

x= 24/2

x= 12

Number of apples = x + 12 ➔ 12+12 = 24 Option (c)

29. Answer: Option (c)

Explanation: We need to take care of two things in order to answer this question. Firstly, the numbers should be consecutive odd numbers. All given options meet this criterion. Secondly, we need to look for the option in which the middle two numbers give us a sum of 24. Only option (c) has numbers such that the sum of middle two is 24 (i.e. 11 + 13 = 24).

30. Answer: Option (b)

Explanation: If we observe closely, we note that every next number in this sequence is obtained by multiplying the previous number by 2. i.e.

48 = 24*2

24= 12*2

12= 6*2

Therefore, in order to find the next number in the sequence, we multiply 48 by 2.

48*2 = 96

31. Answer: Option (a)

Explanation: Please note that it's a tricky question. The perimeter of the rectangular house is given as 44 yards, and the length of the house is given as 36 feet (units are different).

1 yard = 3 feet

44 yards = 132 feet

As we know that the perimeter of the rectangular house equals,

Perimeter = 2*(length) + 2*(width)

132 = 2(36) + 2* width

Width = (132-72)/2 = 30 feet

32. Answer: Option (b)

Explanation: We know that the volume of a cylinder is given by the formula $V = \pi r^2 h$

Important thing to note in this question is that the diameter of the cylinder in given instead of its radius. Also, its given in feet instead of inches. So, we first convert it into inches i.e. 1 foot = 12 inches diameter. So, the radius becomes 12/2 = 6 inches.

Now, putting in the values of radius and height in the formula, we get

$V = (3.14)(6)^2(14) = 1584$ cubic inches.

33. Answer: Option (e)

Explanation: We are given with the width of the cube. As we know that all sides of the cube are equal to each other, we say that the length and height of this cube is also 5.

So, the volume of this cube becomes;

Volume = Length * Width * Height = 5 * 5 * 5 = 125

34. Answer: Option (b)

Explanation: The diameter of the can is given as 3 inches. The radius, therefore, becomes 1.5 (i.e. half of the diameter). Height of the can is given as 8 inches.

Volume = $\pi r^2 h$

$V = (3.14)(1.5)^2(8) = 56.52$ cubic inches

35. Answer: Option (c)

Explanation: The area of this square flower bed is given as 16. This means that when the length and width of this square flowerbed was multiplied, we got 16. Only 4*4 gives us 16. Therefore, we are left with only one option for the length of the each side of this square i.e. 4.

Now, we know that the length of each side of the square flowerbed is 16, Therefore, the perimeter becomes 4+4+4+4 = 16.

Important thing to note in this question is that the flowerbed is a 'square'. If it were a rectangular flowerbed, it could have a perimeter of 16 or 20.

36. Answer: Option (c)

Explanation: From the given information in the question, we know that 25% of the actual price of desk is $45. If we write this in form of an equation, it becomes;

(25/100) * x = $45 (25% of 'x' equals $45)

x= 45/0.25 ➔ $180

Therefore, the actual price of the desk equals to $180.

37. Answer: Option (c)
Explanation: Let's suppose that the actual value of the taxes is 'x'. 8.9% of this value equals $1100. Writing this in form of an equation, we get:
(8.9/100)* x = 1100
x=1100/ 0.089 ➔ $12359

38. Answer: Option (a)
Explanation: We know that:
Interest = Principal Amount * Rate * Time
Putting values in this formula, we get
210 = 3000 * 0.07 * Time
Time = 210/ (3000*0.07) ➔ 1
Therefore, time required = 1 year.

39. Answer: Option (e)
Explanation: Let's suppose that the unknown number is 'x'. So, 35% of 'x' is equal to 70. Writing this in form of an equation,
(35/100)* x = 70
x = 70/0.35
x= 200

40. Answer: Option (b)
Explanation: In order to find 5% of 2000, we need to multiply 2000 by (5/100) i.e.
2000*0.05 = 100

41. Answer: Option (c)
Explanation: We know that:
In this given question, principal amount is $2500, interest is $600, and rate is 0.06.
Interest = Principal Amount * Rate * Time
Putting values in this formula, we get
600 = 2500 * 0.06 * Time
Time = 600/ (2500*0.07) ➔ 4
Therefore, time required = **4 years**.

42. Answer: Option (a)
Explanation: We are given with two equations in this question. Firstly, it's given that r = 5z. Secondly, its given that 15z = 3y, and we are asked about the value of 'r' in terms of 'y'. If we divide the second equation by '3', we get 5z = y, but from the first equation (i.e. r = 5z), we know that 5z = r. So, we conclude that r = 5z = y ➔ r = y

43. Answer: Option(c)
Explanation: This is a tricky question. We need to find 35% of a number but this number is unknown. But we are given with that fact that 12 is 15% of that number. So, we first find out that 12 is 15% of what number? In order to find that out, we write the following equation:
0.15* x = 12
x= 12/0.15 ➔80

Now, we need to find 35% of 80. This can be easily found by multiplying 80 by (35/100) i.e.
80* 0.35 = 28

44. Answer: Option (c)

Explanation: From the statement of the question, it is clear that when we take 20% off the price of computer, it costs $1600. This means that $1600 equals 80% of the actual price of the computer. Writing this in form of an equation;

0.8 * x = $1600

x = 1600/0.8

x = $2000 where 'x' is the actual price of the computer.

45. Answer: Option (b)

Explanation: First of all, you should know that 25% profit on the actual price means that we have multiplied the original price by 1.25 i.e. (1+ 0.25). So, in order to find the actual price of SUV, we divide it by 1.25. This gives us $39000/1.25 ➔ $31200 which is the original price of the SUV.

46. Answer: Option (d)

Explanation: The original price of the dishwasher is given as $450. Since it is on a 15% sale, the price of dishwasher becomes 0.85* 450 = $382.5 [Please note that we have multiplied by 0.85 because this item is on 15% sale. 15% = 0.15. When an item is on 15% sale, it means that you have to pay for 100-15 ➔ 85% of the actual amount] (20% = 0.20)

The person buying this dishwasher is an employee of this store, so he gets an additional 20% discount on this item, So, the final amount which he needs to pay becomes 0.8* 382.5 = $306 [Note that we have multiplied by 0.80 because it is on further 20% sale. When an item is on 20% sale, it means that you have to pay for 100% - 20% ➔ 80% of the actual amount]

47. Answer: Option (d)

Explanation: Hotel chares a tax of 0.3% i.e. 0.3/100 = 0.003. Multiplying it with $55 gives us the amount of tax amount which hotel has charged to this traveler.

$55* 0.003 = $0.165

Note that the given answer choices are in cents and our answer is in dollars. We convert our answer in to cents by multiplying it with 100. It becomes 16.5 cents. The nearest possible option 17 cents which is Option (c).

48. Answer: Option (d)

Explanation: The best way to answer this question is by considering all the answer choices one by one. We start with option (a) and see if it's correct. Grace has a total of 16 jellybeans, and she takes out 4. It is quite possible that she took all the green or all blue jellybeans, and missing out the red colored jellybeans; therefore, option (a) doesn't ensure us that she took out a jellybean of each color. Considering option (b) and (c), we see that even if Grace takes out 8 or 12 jellybeans, she still can't be sure if she has got all colors or not i.e. it is quite possible that she took out all 8 red ones, or may be all 8 red ones and 4 green ones, and still missing out on blue jellybeans.

Thus, in order to be completely sure that she has taken out jellybeans of every color, she must take out at least 13 or more jellybeans. Since we are asked about the minimum number, we choose option (d).

49. Answer: Option (c)

Explanation: This is a tricky question. We are given with the sales tax percentage and the actual amount of the book. First of all, we need to find out the amount we would be charged for this including sales tax, and then we need to subtract it from 100, to find out the change we will receive from them.

8.5% tax on $80 becomes 0.085*80 = $6.8

So, the total amount that we will be charged becomes 80+ 6.8 = $86.8

Subtracting it from $100 to find the change, we get 100 – 86.8 = $13.40

50. Answer: Option (a)

Explanation: From the given information in the question, we get to know that the pens are sold in packs of 6 at \$2.35 per pack, and we need to buy $\frac{240}{6}$ = 40 packs. Therefore, the total amount required for 240 pens is 40*2.35 = \$94.

Also, the staplers are sold in sets of 2 at \$12.95 per set, and we need to buy $\frac{6}{2}$ = 3 sets of staplers.

Therefore, the total amount for staplers equals 3*12.95 = \$38.85

Total cost = \$94 + \$38.85 → \$132.85

51. Answer: Option (b)

Explanation: Let these two cyclists be A and B. Cyclist A is travelling at a speed of 6 miles per hour. Cyclist B is travelling at 10 miles per hour. Cyclist A started cycling 3 hours before cyclist B, so in these 3 hours, he had already travelled 6*3 = 18 miles. Now, lets check the distances covered by each cyclist for every hour.

After 1 Hour →   Cyclist A = 18+6 = 24 miles
               Cyclist B = 10 miles

After 2 Hours →   Cyclist A = 24+6 = 30 miles
               Cyclist B = 10+10 = 20 miles

After 3 Hours →   Cyclist A = 30+6 = 36 miles
               Cyclist B = 20+10 = 30 miles

After 4 Hours →   Cyclist A = 36+6 = 42 miles
               Cyclist B = 30+10 = 40 miles

After 4.5 Hours →   Cyclist A = 42+3 = 45 miles (We have added 3 here because we are
          considering distance covered by cyclist A in half hour i.e. 6/2)
               Cyclist B = 40 + 5 = 45 miles (We have added 5 here because we are
          considering distance covered by cyclist B in half hour i.e. 10/2)
Therefore, after 4.5 hours, both cyclists would have covered the same distance.

52. Answer: Option (b)

Explanation: We need to calculate the individual work rates of each of the three given persons.

Jim can fill the pool in 30 minutes i.e. in one minute, he can fill $\frac{1}{30}$ of the pool.

Sue can fill the pool in 45 minutes i.e. in one minute, Sue can fill $\frac{1}{45}$ of the pool.

Tony can fill the pool in $1\frac{1}{2}$ hour [90 minutes], i.e. in one minute, he can fill $\frac{1}{90}$ of the pool.

So, if Jim, Sue and Tony work together for 1 minute, they can fill $\frac{1}{30} + \frac{1}{45} + \frac{1}{90} = \frac{1}{15}$ of the pool.
Therefore, in order to fill the pool completely working together, they would need 15 minutes.

53. Answer: Option (d)

Explanation: In a given sample of 100 women aged over 35, 8 have been married at least twice. In order to find out the number of women at least married twice, in a sample of 5000 women, we write the following ratio:

Sample Space :	Aged Above 35
100-women :	8 married at least twice
5000-women :	'x' married at least twice

Cross multiplying, we get x*100 = 8*5000

x =40000/100 ➔ 400

54. Answer: Option (e)

Explanation: The total distance which needs to be covered is 28 miles. Total time which John has to reach there is 30 minutes i.e. 0.5 hour.

As we know that speed $= \frac{Distance}{Time} = \frac{28\ miles}{0.5\ hours} = 56$ miles/hour

55. Answer: Option (a)

Explanation: Steven can mix 20 drinks in 5 minutes, which means that in one minute, he can mix $\frac{20}{5} = 4$ drinks.

Sue can mix 20 drinks in 10 minutes which means that Sue can mix $\frac{20}{10} = 2$ drinks per minute.

Jack can mix 20 drinks in 15 minutes which means that he can mix $\frac{20}{15} = 1.33$ drinks per minute.

Therefore, if Steven, Sue and Jack work together for one minute, they can mix 4+2+1.33 = 7.33 drinks per minutes. In order to mix a total of 20 drinks working together, they will need $\frac{20}{7.33} = 2.72$ minutes.

In order to find the exact seconds, we multiply our answer by 60. This gives us 60*2.72 = 163.7 seconds. We know that 163.7 correspond to 2 minutes and 44 seconds (approx).

56. Answer: Option (d)

Explanation: From the statement of the question, it is clear that we need string that is at least 40 inches long (i.e. 36 inch waist and 4 inches for knot) but not longer than 42 inches.

Let's examine the length of strings available in answer options.

Option (a) = 3 feet = 36 inches Incorrect

Option (b) = 3(3/4) feet = 45 inches Incorrect

Option (c) = 3(1/2) feet = 42 inches Incorrect

Option (d) = 3 (1/4) feet = 40 inches **Correct**

Option (e) = 2(1/2) feet = 30 inches Incorrect

57. Answer: Option (a)

Explanation: In order to find the percentage change, we use the following formula.

Percentage Change $= \frac{Final\ value - Original\ Value}{Original\ Value} *100$

Therefore, percentage increase becomes, $\frac{19-12}{12} *100 = 58\%$

58. Answer: Option (c)

Explanation: It's a tricky question. First of all, you must note that one plane is flying toward north, and the other one is flying towards west. The total distance between these two cannot be calculated by simply adding their individual distances. We need to use Pythagoras theorem to solve this question. Both airplanes left the airport at same time 1:00 pm and we looking for how much apart they would be after two hours at 3:00 pm.

Plane flying toward north has a speed of 150 miles per hour, so in two hours, it would have covered 300 miles.

Plane flying towards west has a speed of 200 miles per hours, so it would have covered 400 miles in two hours.

Using Pythagoras Theorem, We find the distance between these two planes as:

Distance = $\sqrt{(300)^2 + (400)^2}$ = 500 miles

59. Answer: Option (e)

Explanation: The number of people on Thursday is 345. Every next day the number of people triples.

On Friday, it becomes 3*345 = 1035

On Saturday, the number of people who came to this festival became 3 * 1035 =3105

On Sunday, the number of people who came to this festival became 3 * 3105 = 9315

60. Answer: Option (a)

Explanation: It is important to note that the rate of the carpet is given is per sq. yard and the dimensions of the room are given in feet. So, we need to convert the width and length of the room in yards, and then calculate the total area of the room. We know that 1 foot = 0.33 yards

10 feet = 3.33 yards

12 feet = 4 yards

Area of the room = 4*3.33 = 13.32 sq yards

So, the total cost to carpet this room equals 13.32 * 12.51 ➔ $166.6

61. Answer: Option (d)

Explanation: First of all, we add the inches, feet and yards individually.

Inches: 6 + 5+ 8 = 19 inches

Feet = 2 + 1 + 2 = 5 Feet

Yards = 1 + 2 + 4 = 7 yards

As we know that there are 12 inches in 1 foot, so 19 inches becomes 1 foot and 7 inches. Therefore, we add one more to 5 feet, which makes it 6 feet.

Also, we know that 1 foot = 0.33 yards, so 6 feet = 2 yards.

This makes the total length equal to 9 yards and 7 inches. [9 yards because 7 yards calculated in the first step plus 2 yards from 6 feet conversion to yards.]

62. Answer: Option (b)

Explanation: The amount of calcium actually required was 500 mg in that vitamin, but it has lost 325mg of calcium in it. Therefore, it has got 500-325 = 175 mg calcium left in it after expiration.

63. Answer: Option (c)

Explanation: There are 4mg of medication in 5 mL dose. We need to give 20 mg to the patient and $\frac{20}{4} = 5$ so we multiply the dose by 5 to give our desired amount of medication to the patient. Therefore, $5*5mL = 25$ mL

64. Answer: Option (c)

Explanation: We know that the volume is given my formula length* width * height. In order to find the correct volume of the aquariums given in the answer options, we multiply their respective length, width and heights to see, which on equals to 1680.

Option (a) = 12*12*12 = 1728

Option (b) = 13*15*16 = 3120

Option (c) = 14*20*6 = 1680 which is our required answer. No need to check further options.

65. Answer: Option (b)

Explanation: If she takes the business courses, her salary would increase from $12000 to $14000. We know that

Percentage Change $= \frac{Final\ value - Original\ Value}{Original\ Value}*100$ ➜ $\frac{14000-12000}{12000}*100$

$\frac{2000}{12000}*100 = 16.7\%$

66. Answer: Option (d)

Explanation: His new hourly salary would become $15.50+$0.75 = $16.25

Percentage change $= \frac{Final\ value - Original\ Value}{Original\ Value}*100$

$\frac{16.25-15.50}{15.50}*100$

$\frac{0.75}{15.50}*100 = 4.8\%$

67. Answer: Option (e)

Explanation: Price of Edmond's car was $49000 but he had to sell it at 20% less. This means that the price at which he sold his car was 80% of the actual price. Therefore,

0.8*49000 = $39200

68. Answer: Option (b)

Explanation: The easiest way to solve these types of questions is to imagine a constant number. Let's say there are 100 people in the fish fry company, such that one half of the people are employee i.e. 100/2 = 50 employees.

Similarly, the spouses of the employees make one third of the attendance i.e. $\frac{100}{3} = 33.3$

Now, the remaining people are 100- 50 – 33.3 = 16.7 %

(Note: It is not possible that there are 33.3 or 16.7 person in the restraint. The number of people is always a whole number. But in this case while solving this question, we have used percentage approximation)

69. Answer: Option (b)

Explanation: First of all, we need to calculate the individual work rate for each of the given persons.

Sam can do that job in 4 days means that he can do ¼ of that job in a single day.

Lisa can do that same job in 6 days means that she can complete $\frac{1}{6}$ of the job in one day.

Tom can complete that job in 2 days, means that he can complete ½ of that job in one day.

So, if Sam, Lisa, and Tom work together for one day, they can complete $(\frac{1}{4} + \frac{1}{6} + \frac{1}{2}) = 0.917$ job in a single day.
In order to complete 1 job working together, they would need 1/0.917 = 1.09 Days

70. Answer: Option (c)
Explanation: Cake requires $\frac{3}{8} = 0.375$ cup of sugar, whereas, cookies require $\frac{3}{5} = 0.6$ cup of sugar. This makes a total of 0.375+0.6 = 0.975 cup of sugar.
Sarah has got $\frac{15}{16} = 0.9375$ cup of sugar.
Therefore, it is clear that Sarah needs more sugar than she already has got. The exact amount of sugar required can be calculated by subtracting total sugar from required sugar.
i.e. 0.975-0.9375 = 0.0375
Therefore, Option (c) is correct. $[\frac{3}{80} = 0.0375]$

71. Answer: Option (d)
First find the length of side AB. AB = $\sqrt{(17-5)2 + (8-3)2}$ = 13.
If AB = 13, then A_{square} = 132 = 169.
AB is also the diameter of the circle, so A $_{circle}$ π ($d^2/4$) = 169 π /4.
The area outside the circle, but within the square is:
A $_{square}$ − A $_{circle}$ = 169(1- π /4).

72. Answer: Option (a)
The Pythagorean triple (special right triangle property) means the two shorter sides form a right triangle.
1/2bh = A.
(1/2)(3)(4) = 6.

73. Answer: Option (e)
AB^2 = AC^2 = AD2 + CD^2 → AB^2 = 3^2 + 4^2 → AB = 5.

74. Answer: Option (a)
In a right triangle, the square of the hypotenuse = the sum of the squares of the other two sides. AB^2 + BC^2 = AC^2 → AC^2 = 36 + 64 → AC = 10.

75. Answer: Option (c)
If the area of the square is 36 cm^2, then each side is 6 cm. If we look at the triangle made by half the square, that diagonal would be the hypotenuse of the triangle, and its length = $\sqrt{6^2+6}$ ^{2} = 6√2.
This hypotenuse is also the diameter of the circle, so the radius of the circle is 3√2.
The area of the circle =$A = \pi r^2$= 18π.
The area outside the square, but within the circle is 18π -36.

Chapter 5: Final Thoughts

In the end, we know that you will be successful in taking the ASVAB. Although the process can be challenging, if you continue with hard work and dedication, you will find that your efforts will pay off.

If you are struggling after reading this book and following our guidelines, we sincerely hope that you will take note of our advice and seek additional help.

Start by asking friends about the resources that they are using. If you are still not reaching the score you want, consider getting the help of a tutor.

We wish you the best of luck and happy studying.

Most importantly, we honor your decision to join the armed forces – you put a lot of work into getting there, and your efforts and drive are more than admirable.

Sincerely,
The Accepted, Inc. Team

Made in the USA
San Bernardino, CA
30 April 2015